W9-BKE-957

DISCERNING
the Voice of
GOD

DISCERNING
the Voice of
GOD

HOW TO RECOGNIZE WHEN GOD SPEAKS

Priscilla Shirer

MOODY PUBLISHERS

CHICAGO

© 2007 by
PRISCILLA SHIRER

All rights reserved. No part of this book may be reproduced in any form without permission in writing from the publisher, except in the case of brief quotations embodied in critical articles or reviews.

All Scripture quotations, unless otherwise indicated, are taken from the *Holy Bible, New Living Translation*, copyright © 1996. Used by permission of Tyndale House Publishers, Inc., Wheaton, Illinois 60189. All rights reserved.

Scripture quotations marked NKJV are taken from the *New King James Version*. Copyright © 1982 by Thomas Nelson, Inc. Used by permission. All rights reserved.

Scripture quotations marked NIV are taken from the *Holy Bible, New International Version*®. NIV®. Copyright © 1973, 1978, 1984 by International Bible Society. Used by permission of Zondervan. All rights reserved.

Scripture quotations marked CEV are taken from the *Contemporary English Version*. Copyright © 1991, 1992, 1995 by American Bible Society. Used by permission.

Scripture quotations marked NASB are taken from the *New American Standard Bible*®, Copyright © 1960, 1962, 1963, 1968, 1971, 1972, 1973, 1975, 1977, 1995 by The Lockman Foundation. Used by permission. (www.Lockman.org)

Scripture quotations marked AMP are taken from *The Amplified Bible*. Copyright © 1965, 1987 by The Zondervan Corporation. *The Amplified New Testament* copyright © 1958, 1987 by The Lockman Foundation. Used by permission.

Scripture quotations marked *The Message* are from *The Message*, copyright © by Eugene H. Peterson 1993, 1994, 1995. Used by permission of NavPress Publishing Group.

All italicized Scripture is the author's emphasis.

Cover Design: The DesignWorksGroup
Cover Image: Steve Gardner, Pixelworks Studio
Interior Design: Ragonts Design
Editor: Peg Short

Library of Congress Cataloging-in-Publication Data

Shirer, Priscilla Evans.
  Discerning the voice of God : how to recognize when God speaks / Priscilla Shirer.
     p. cm.
  ISBN-10: 0-8024-5009-1
  ISBN-13: 978-0-8024-5009-8
  1. God (Christianity)—Knowableness. 2. Spiritual life—Christianity. 3. Spirituality.
  4. Listening--Religious aspects—Christianity. 5. Prayer—Christianity. 6. Private revelations.
  I. Title.

BT103.S445 2007
231.7—dc22
                                                            2006035755

We hope you enjoy this book from Moody Publishers. Our goal is to provide high-quality, thought-provoking books and products that connect truth to your real needs and challenges. For more information on other books and products written and produced from a biblical perspective, go to www.moodypublishers.com or write to:

Moody Publishers
820 N. LaSalle Boulevard
Chicago, IL 60610

5 7 9 10 8 6 4

Printed in the United States of America

Jerry, this is for you.
You've taught me how to wait patiently to hear God's voice.
Thank you for giving me time to listen for the sighs of the supernatural
and for helping me know how to hear, discern, and obey.

Contents

Foreword

What could be more important in the midst of our busy, complicated lives than being able to discern the voice of the Almighty? Priscilla Shirer is on target as she inspires us all to listen so we can be blessed! This is a subject so often overlooked in contemporary Christian literature. Confusion and frustration will result when other voices drown out God's leading. You will be blessed by the balance outlined by the author between God's eternal word and the present day ministry of the Holy Spirit. I thank God for this book and the beautiful spirit in which it was written. Read it and be blessed!

—Jim Cymbala
Senior Pastor, The Brooklyn Tabernacle

Acknowledgments

To my grandparents: both sets—who are all still living and growing younger every year as you are continually renewed by the Spirit of God. Thank you for showing me what it means to live while listening to and walking with God. If you get to see Him first, tell Him that I'm coming.

To the Moody Family: Thank you for continuing to allow me to partner with you. I am so blessed to work with people who know how to walk the distinct, yet often fine line between business and ministry. Thanks for having a true heart for the Lord and remembering what this is really all about.

To Peg Short: God brought you to me just in the nick of time! Thank you for helping me shape my thoughts and written work into this carefully crafted manuscript. This book would not be clear to the reader apart from the great work you have done. Thank you for so passionately sticking to the integrity of the message on my heart. I am so grateful not only to call you my partner, but more importantly, my friend. Can't wait to do it again!

Just Between Us

riend, I have a confession.

I've been a believer for many years, and I spent most of that time not hearing God's voice. I read in the Bible about people to whom He spoke, and I heard from modern-day believers how God spoke to them. But I rarely, if ever, experienced that kind of connection with Him. I never expected the God of the universe to really speak to me about the personal details of my life. Hearing God's voice was for other people, not for me.

Sound familiar?

I meet many believers who love the Lord and live holy lives, yet they still seem to be missing something in their Christian experience. They don't feel God's presence, hear His voice, or experience His power. Since you've picked up this book, I suspect that may be true for you as well.

For the record, I've come a long way. As I've matured in my faith, I've come to know God better. And the more intimate I've become with Him, the more acquainted I've become with His voice. With all the confidence I have, I can assure you that God does speak. The best personal proof I have of this is that *He spoke to me just this morning!* I'm learning that if my spiritual ears are open, the same voice that called me into His marvelous light speaks to me day by day.

The Bible declares that God is the same "yesterday, today, and forever" (Hebrews 13:8). This means that the same God who spoke with the prophets of old also speaks with His saints today. The conversational nature of our relationship with the Almighty makes our faith unique. The Old Testament says that what distinguished the Israelites' faith from all others was that they heard God's voice (Deuteronomy 4:33). And the apostle Paul reminds us that the difference between the relationship we have with the true God and the relationship pagans have with their idols is that their gods are "speechless" (1 Corinthians 12:2).

Our faith isn't based on rules and regulations but on sweet fellowship with our God. One of the clearest promises we have in Scripture of God speaking to His children is found in John 10:27, "My sheep hear my voice; I know them, and they follow me." God clearly wants our relationship with Him to be intimate and interactive.

My friend, if God's Son died for you, don't you think He would move heaven and earth to stay in touch with you? When Jesus walked on earth, He willingly revealed Himself to everyone around Him, even though He knew that many would reject Him. The beauty of our relationship with Him is that He *desires* to speak to us. He places a high priority on this because it's crucial to the kind of relationship He wants to have with us.

If that's true, why do we so often not expect to hear from God today? Simple. If God wants us to hear His voice, the Father of Lies is going to do everything he can to make us think that we *aren't* hearing it. When we hear from God, we call it intuition, coincidence, or even luck—anything but what it is: the voice of God. We're so used to dismissing His voice that we've convinced ourselves that He no longer speaks to His children. But the Bible says over and over that God *does* speak to us. We *are* hearing from Him. We just may not know it's Him.

It can be a continual struggle to know for sure when we are hearing God's voice. So often our traditions, desires, guilt, and even our own ego can drown out His voice. So how can we discern His voice from the Enemy's and even from our own? And how can we know when God is speaking?

That's what *Discerning God's Voice* is about. My goal is to assist you on your journey, just as others have helped me, by telling me what God has shown them. I want you to know that you can clearly hear from God, and I want to help you learn to recognize His voice, so you will know for sure when He is the one speaking.

Just to be clear, this book can't give you a formula for discerning God's voice with 100 percent accuracy. All of the mature, godly believers I have spoken with have told me that discerning God's voice is something they still don't always get right. None of us will ever completely master this while we're on earth and still clothed in this old flesh. Nevertheless, it's a skill we can—and must—learn.

This book can help you do that by capturing the sound of God's voice and learning to discern it through His character, His Spirit, and His Word. The way in which God chooses to speak may change, and the way saints hear His voice might differ, but the characteristics of His voice will not. His voice is different from any other, and the more acquainted you become with the sound of His voice, the more clearly you'll be able to recognize when He is speaking.

Throughout *Discerning God's Voice*, you'll hear God speaking through His written Word, the Bible. You will also hear how God has spoken to saints through the ages and how they've learned to recognize His voice. Some of the things you'll hear from them come from books they've written; others were written especially for this book. Wanting to know how God's faithful servants know when they're hearing God's voice, I wrote to many brothers and sisters in Christ and asked them that question. A different saint's answer appears at the end of each chapter.

Friend, I would like to ask you that question as well. How do you know for sure when God is speaking to you? If you are a Christian, but can't answer that question right now, this book can help you learn to recognize God's voice. I pray that it will challenge you, encourage you, and better equip you to discern the magnificent voice of our great God.

—PRISCILLA SHIRER

PART ONE

Hearing God's Voice

"Call to Me and I will answer you, and I will tell you great and mighty things, which you do not know."

—JEREMIAH 33:3 (NASB)

They stood with Jesus on a mountainside. Perhaps they thought this would be just like all of the other times when they had met with the Savior. But Peter, James, and John were about to behold something extraordinary. As they watched in amazement, Jesus' clothes began to glow and His face shone like the sun. Suddenly two figures appeared with Jesus: Moses and Elijah. In this divine moment, God the Father spoke from heaven and said, "This is my beloved Son, and I am fully pleased with him. Listen to him" (Matthew 17:5).

Of all of the things that God the Father could have said, He said, "Listen." He didn't say, "Ask" or "Inquire" or even "Serve" Him. He said, "Listen to him."

This command remains true even today. We are called to listen to Him because He desires to speak to us and He has important, specific things to say to you.

God can and will speak. But do you really believe He will talk to you? And do you anticipate that the divine Word of God can be heard by you? God wants you to know His will and direction for your life. Listen and He will speak. Wait and expect His voice and you will hear Him.

A Saint Speaks

"Those who do not believe God speaks specifically will simply ignore or explain away all the times when God does communicate with them. However, those who spend each day in a profound awareness that God does speak are in a wonderful position to receive His word."

—A. W. TOZER

1

Expect to Hear

"Wait and hope for and expect the Lord; be
brave and of good courage and let your heart
be stout and enduring. Yes, wait for and hope
for and expect the Lord."

—PSALM 27:14 (AMP)

I sat on the set of a live television broadcast at the CBS af-
filiate in Dallas. Fresh out of college, I was anxious and ner-
vous about the demands this new job would require. I had
never hosted a live show before. Without the safety net that
taping provides, I was concerned I would not be able to
smoothly conduct an entire show. What if I lost my train of
thought or didn't know what I was supposed to do next?
Seeing my apprehension, the producer emerged from the
sound booth, walked over, and fitted me with a small device
that tucked comfortably around my ear. She explained that
this tiny piece of equipment, affectionately known in media
circles as "the ear," would keep me connected to her throughout the show. At any time during the program, she could speak

to me, providing direction and guidance. Although I was unaware of all the nuances of live television, she was a pro and knew exactly what information to give me at each stage of the broadcast.

When you became a Christian, you were fitted with "the ear." The Holy Spirit has been given to you, so that you are continually connected to the One who can give you clear and consistent guidance for your life. If you are expecting to hear Him, He can calm your anxieties as you trust Him for specific direction.

Yet as I've looked back on my own experience and have spoken with Christians from all walks of life, I've discovered that many of us don't really believe God will speak to us about the details of our lives. We claim to believe it, but secretly we're discouraged because we can't discern God's voice. We don't doubt that God *can* speak; we just doubt that He will speak *to us.*

A couple of years ago, I needed a very specific healing. As I searched for a solution, the Holy Spirit convicted me that I was seeking help from everyone except the Lord. I hadn't even asked Him to speak to me about it. I had asked for advice and medication from doctors and sought guidance from Internet sites and books, but I hadn't laid my request before God. As I searched my heart as to why I hadn't prayed about it, I quickly discovered two reasons.

First, I didn't truly expect the Lord to speak to me. I didn't anticipate that He would enter my world with a practical, personal, life-changing word. Second, I didn't expect the Lord to heal me. Based on the miracles described in the New Testament, my *mind* knew that the Lord is able to heal. I had even seen and heard of Him healing modern-day believers. But in the deep recesses of my heart, I didn't really believe that He would heal *me.*

Fortunately, my Bible study took me to the book of Habakkuk. God used that little book to teach me an important lesson: God's voice is responsive. And discerning it begins when we listen in anticipation, expecting to hear from Him.

A SAINT SPEAKS: *"If we come to Him doubting His ability to speak, we will have a difficult time listening. So we must come expectantly."*

—CHARLES STANLEY

Come Expecting

Habakkuk was a man in great despair, desperate to hear from God. He was appalled at the sinful behavior of the people of Judah and couldn't understand why God wasn't doing something about it. He had prayed and prayed, but God didn't seem to be listening. If He was, He wasn't answering. So Habakkuk cried, "How long, O Lord, will I call for help, and You will not hear? I cry out to You, 'Violence!' Yet You do not save. Why do You make me see iniquity, and cause me to look on wickedness?" (Habakkuk 1:2–3 NASB).

Although the discouraged prophet expected God to answer him, he had two fundamental questions: "How long?" and "Why?" These two questions probably sound very familiar. When the circumstances of life seem to be closing in on us and we see no end in sight, we want to know how long we will have to continue calling out to God and why He doesn't do something about our situation.

We don't know how long Habakkuk had been calling out to God, but he had most likely been at it for quite a while, because by then he was pointing an accusatory finger at God. Finally, God answered the prophet with these words: "Look among the nations! Observe! Be astonished! Wonder! Because I am doing something in your days" (v. 5 NASB).

Instead of responding directly to Habakkuk's complaint, God encouraged him to look around and see what was happening. God basically said, "I *am* speaking and I *am* doing something. You've been looking through the wrong lenses so you just don't hear or see it."

God's reply to Habakkuk was intended to restore the prophet's confidence in Him. He wanted Habakkuk to recognize His activity so that he would continue to expect Him to come through for him, despite what he was facing. While the prophet was waiting for God to answer, God was already answering! Habakkuk just needed to be fitted with spiritual vision in order to become aware of it. God is always speaking and moving, even when He seems silent.

At the time I studied this passage, I was making the transition to motherhood. I must admit that it has been one of the most difficult challenges in my life so far. Like most moms, I have been brought to tears and very often to my knees before the Lord. In those moments, God's reply to Habakkuk encouraged me.

As I have taken to heart God's command to look and watch, I have begun to see God's hand where I hadn't before. With spiritual vision, I now can see that God is using my children to produce the fruit of the Spirit in me, something for which I have fervently prayed. I can see how the Lord is using them to temper me and make me more fully into the woman He wants me to be. Seeing what God is up to has restored my confidence that He is speaking and working in my situation.

If you have been asking God for help, but feel that He hasn't been responding, pray that He will help you see the things you might be missing that He is already doing in your life. This will encourage you to anticipate His word to you.

To discern God's voice and see Him working, we must approach Him expectantly and confidently. He isn't idle or insensitive to our requests, and He will respond.

> **A SAINT SPEAKS:** *"Risk being honest, and expect His insight in return. Take time to be still before Him. Decide to seek the Lord until you find Him."*
>
> —BRUCE WILKINSON

Come as You Are

When God spoke to Habakkuk, He told the prophet what He was up to: He was preparing the Babylonians to discipline Judah for its sin.

Why do you think God waited so long to have this conversation with Habakkuk? Perhaps the answer is found at the end of verse 5 (NASB)—because "you would not believe if you were told." God knew that Habakkuk would find His message *hard to believe.*

Sure enough, Habakkuk couldn't believe what God was planning to do. Maybe he hadn't heard Him right, or maybe God hadn't even spoken at all! How could the God he knew be planning to use the vilest nation on earth to punish His own people?

Habakkuk continued his conversation with God by questioning the wisdom of His divine plan: "Your eyes are too pure to approve evil, and You can not look on wickedness with favor," he said. "Why," then, "do You look with favor on those who deal treacherously? Why are You silent when the wicked swallow up those more righteous than they?" (v.13 NASB).

Before we come down too hard on Habakkuk for questioning God, we need to remember that Job did this as well. So did Jeremiah (Jeremiah 32:25) and Jonah (Jonah 4:2). So have I and probably so have you.

> **HE SPEAKS:** *"My thoughts are completely different from yours," says the Lord. "And my ways are far beyond anything you could imagine."*
>
> —ISAIAH 55:8

Some people think that believers should never question God. But it's clear from Scripture and our own experience that we do—and that it doesn't keep God from speaking to us. He always responds in His own timing. Even when we have great thoughts about God, we cannot always understand His ways. Despite that, He still desires to make Himself known to the seeking heart.

Sometimes God doesn't answer us right away for the same reason He didn't answer Habakkuk right away. He knows that His message will be hard for us to believe, because it won't match our expectations. We aren't going to want to believe what He says, and we will use what we know about His character to convince ourselves that He can't really mean it.

God is gracious, and when we want to speak to Him, He invites us to come as we are—questioning, complaining, and confused. When we approach Him, praising Him for what we already know about Him, He will use our questions to reveal more about Himself and enlarge our understanding. Since our relationship is meant to be reciprocal, we must also allow Him to come as He is—wiser than we can comprehend.

> **A SAINT SPEAKS:** *"If you want to hear God's voice clearly and you are uncertain, then remain in His presence until He changes this uncertainty. Often much can happen during this waiting on the Lord. Sometimes He changes pride into humility; doubt into faith and peace; sometimes lust into purity. The Lord can and will do it."*
>
> —CORRIE TEN BOOM

Come Determined to Wait

Once Habakkuk's confidence was restored, he still had questions, but now he was prepared to wait for the answers. As he finished speaking, he had an uneasy feeling that God was going to rebuke him for questioning Him, but he was still determined to hear what God had to say. "I will stand at my watch and station myself on the ramparts; I will look to see what he will say to me, and what answer I am to give to this complaint" (Habakkuk 2:1 NIV).

The Hebrew words for *stand* and *station* are military terms. Habakkuk's use of them reminds me of the guards outside England's Buckingham Palace. Those guys refuse to move no matter what happens. Tourists (like me) have been known to make faces at them and do all sorts of things to try to distract them, but they don't bat an eye. They don't move a muscle. They know what they've been assigned to do, and they won't allow themselves to be distracted.

Habakkuk's posture was militant; his stance strong; his resolve sure. He was on the lookout. He expected God to answer and was determined to wait until He did.

HE SPEAKS: *"Listen to my voice in the morning, Lord. Each morning I bring my requests to you and wait expectantly."*

—PSALM 5:3

We will always wait for things that are important to us. We'll stay by our phone waiting for a call about a job opportunity or a report from a doctor's office. We'll wait in line for groceries or a roller-coaster ride. We are willing to wait for the excitement-filled days and weeks before our wedding and the nine long months for a baby to arrive. The value we place on something is in direct proportion to the amount of time we're willing to wait for it.

Hearing God's voice was such a priority in Habakkuk's life that he was willing to be patient. Because he truly expected God to speak, he was able to confidently wait for His word. If we value hearing from God as much as he did, and if we are equally as certain that we will hear His voice, we will be determined to wait patiently for God to speak. There is a direct correlation between your level of anticipation to hear from God and your willingness to wait.

I must admit that waiting to hear from God is difficult for me. But I've begun to see that the process of waiting for a message from God is often just as important as the message itself. As I wait, my faith grows. The waiting prepares me to receive the message that's coming and to respond in obedience. In some cases, the intimacy that I develop with God while waiting *is* the message.

My friend and mentor Anne Graham Lotz once said to me, "I never make a major decision, especially one that will affect another person, before I have received direction from God." She said that for every major decision she has made, there's a specific Scripture verse she can point to as the one God used to personally direct it. Anne so anticipates an answer from God that she is resolved to wait on Him for guidance before coming to a final decision on any matter. What sound advice from a godly woman!

A SAINT SPEAKS: *"Conversing with the Father is colored by the needs of the day. Let your prayer be something definite, arising either out of the Word which you have read, or out of the real soul needs which you long to be satisfied. Let your prayer be so definite that you can say as you go out, 'I know what I have asked from my Father, and I expect an answer.'"*

—ANDREW MURRAY

I wish that I had been prepared to wait for the Lord to speak before I made one decision recently, but I was far too impatient. My friend Rachel had just come to my home to show me a Bible study she was working on to help women make their home a sanctuary. The Lord has gifted her as an interior decorator and given her a passion to share with others the beauty of the home. Rachel showed me the cover she had designed for what would be a twelve-week Bible study, video series, journal, and gift booklet. I looked on in growing excitement at what she had already accomplished, and when she asked me to be her coauthor for the project, I jumped at the chance. I didn't even ask God what He thought. Right then and there, I told her I was in. She could count on me.

But after I had written the introductory chapters and sent them to the publisher, the Lord began to clearly impress upon me through my personal Bible study that I had made a mistake. He had another project I was to be working on at that time. He wanted me to share a message with women about hearing His voice, but my impulsive behavior had put His will on the back burner.

I was so ashamed to have to call Rachel after a couple months of hard work to tell her that I couldn't partner with her on her Bible study. I would have saved myself that embarrassment if I would have simply sought the Lord's guidance and waited on His response before I committed to the project.

Maybe you have been in a similar situation. Perhaps you impulsively got involved in something before you asked for God's opinion and waited for a clear answer. I know many women who get married, move to a different state, or make a career change or important financial decision before they hear from God, only to find out that they would have been much better off if they had just been patient and waited for the Lord to speak.

If you have trouble waiting to hear God, ask yourself, "Do I *really* believe He will speak to the practical personal issues of my life?"

When Habakkuk questioned the wisdom of God's plan, he expected not just an answer but a reprimand. Instead God continued the dialogue with the prophet by reassuring him. Although He would use the wicked Babylonians to punish Judah, He would someday judge them for their sins as well. Habakkuk didn't need to worry. God would see to it that justice was done. Babylon's time was coming.

> **HE SPEAKS:** *"The word they heard did not profit them, because it was not united by faith in those who heard."*
>
> —HEBREWS 4:2 (NASB)

As long as Habakkuk's approach to God was doubtful or accusatory, God had to build the prophet's faith by showing him that He was indeed up to something and then convince him that it was something good. You might say that God had to make a believer out of him. And He did.

God told Habakkuk that his part in the divine plan was to "run with it" (2:2 NIV) and "live by his faith" (2:4 NIV). Faith is the catalyst that allows us to experience God in our everyday lives. Believers who go to God expecting to hear His voice won't hesitate to move forward in obedience when He speaks. That's because they know that the results will always be so astounding that they will be *hard to believe.*

God's words enlarged Habakkuk's perspective and strengthened his faith. Now he no longer pointed an accusatory finger at God or questioned Him. By the time God had finished speaking, Habakkuk could face the future certain that God would not only continue to speak to him but also continually act on his behalf. God was wise and good and just, and

Habakkuk could trust Him completely. Habakkuk's final prayer is full of confidence, faith, and joy:

"Though the fig tree should not blossom and there be no fruit on the vines, though the yield of the olive should fail and the fields produce no food, though the flock should be cut off from the fold and there be no cattle in the stalls, yet I will exult in the Lord, I will rejoice in the God of my salvation" (Habakkuk 3:17–18 NASB).

> **HE SPEAKS:** *"Trust in the Lord with all your heart; do not depend on your own understanding. Seek his will in all you do, and he will direct your paths."*
>
> —PROVERBS 3:5–6

Throughout Scripture, God paints a picture of His relationship with us as one in which He speaks to us as His beloved children and acts on our behalf. Biblical characters didn't call to God and then walk away despondent because they assumed He wasn't going to answer. On the contrary, they waited expectantly and eagerly for God's reply.

This biblical pattern shows not only that God responds, but also that we should eagerly anticipate His response. We can come to Him with great anticipation because we serve a great God. He will never disappoint the believing expectations of those who patiently wait to hear His responsive voice.

HOW DO YOU KNOW IT'S GOD'S VOICE?

"I know when the Lord is speaking to me because literally the air around me changes. There is a stillness that settles all my raging emotions and questions and simply bids me to be silent, listen, and consider what I hear. And then it's almost as if it comes from the center of my being—the answer, the revelation, the instruction, and it is sealed in this definite place inside of me that I can't describe. I only know that I must do what I've been prompted to do. If I resist, I can't breathe, but when I say yes and obey, the most incredible sense of knowing and peace overtakes me, and the matter is settled once and for all."

—MICHELLE MCKINNEY HAMMOND

2

Listen to Him

"Go near to listen . . . Do not be quick with your mouth, do not be hasty in your heart to utter anything before God. God is in heaven and you are on earth, so let your words be few."

—ECCLESIASTES 5:1–2 (NIV)

His name is Elmo. I don't know what it is about that red furry little critter that keeps my kids so intrigued. Maybe if I dyed my hair red and grew some fur, my boys might pay that kind of attention to me too.

When our family is traveling and Jerry and I need to keep the boys occupied, so we can talk, we pop an *Elmo* episode into the DVD player of our SUV. My little guys sit with their eyes glued on the screen, absorbing every word. They don't want to miss anything their hero has to say. On occasion our adult conversation gets too loud. When that happens, the boys sit forward in their car seats and say, "Daddy, please turn it up. We can't hear!"

Jerry's response is always the same: "Are your ears wide open? Why don't you try opening up your ears?" Jackson and Jerry Jr. immediately grab their ear lobes and try to stretch their ears to their fullest capacity. I always turn around to watch as they try to get their ears to open wider.

When they've finished making this adjustment, their father asks them, "Can you hear better now?" They nod their heads and go back to watching Elmo. The volume hasn't changed a bit, but all of a sudden both of them can hear clearly. The reason is quite simple: they have focused on listening.

Have you ever sat forward in your chair and said, "God, please turn up the volume. I can't hear You!" The Father hears our plea and responds with an eternal answer, *"Come to me with your ears wide open. Listen . . ."* (Isaiah 55:3).

God's voice is selective. Most often He chooses to speak to those He knows will listen. This is God's word to you today. He is asking you to focus on listening to Him. Right now, pull on your spiritual earlobes. Take time to listen to God and discipline yourself to discern His voice through prayer, meditation, and worship. This will stretch your capacity to hear what He has to say to you. God always speaks loudly and clearly enough for wide-open ears to hear.

> **HE SPEAKS:** *"Let the wise listen and add to their learning, and let the discerning get guidance."*
>
> —PROVERBS 1:5 (NIV)

Take Time to Listen

I'm pretty bold. When I see men and women whose relationship with the Lord I admire, I'm not afraid to walk right up and ask them what they attribute it to. Without fail, they all say that they deliberately carve out time to be still and listen for God's voice. They spend time with the Lord in prayer in their secret place, listening in silence for Him to speak. As I pondered the prayer life of such believers, I asked myself why my own prayers often seemed so powerless. It became apparent that listening prayer was the missing component.

I invited my friend Jada out for a quick lunch recently, because I needed her advice on a problem. Both very busy, we managed to clear one hour on our calendars to meet. As soon as we arrived, I began to share my concern. I talked incessantly from the beginning of our lunch to the end, explaining every detail. My sweet friend nodded her head and listened sympathetically. When we'd finally eaten our last bite, I paused for a breath and waited for her response. Instead my friend glanced at her watch and then picked up her purse, signaling she needed to leave. "Wait," I said, "I needed your advice. Why haven't you given it to me?" She smiled kindly and said, "Priscilla, I had many things to say, but you never stopped talking long enough to listen."

As I drove home that day pondering her response, the Holy Spirit spoke to me with piercing conviction. How many times had I approached God in the same way? When I considered my prayer life, it was clear why I often came away feeling empty. Like Jada, God reminds me, "I have many things to say to you, Prisiclla, but you haven't taken time to listen."

To be able to discern when God is speaking, we must deliberately turn our attention inward to consider how the Spirit is working in our conscience and causing Scripture to resonate in our hearts. This is what it means to truly listen.

HE SPEAKS: *"Let all my words sink deep into your own heart first. Listen to them carefully for yourself."*

—EZEKIEL 3:10

According to Ecclesiastes 5:2, our "words should be few." This seems to imply we should spend more time listening than talking. Perhaps that's why God gave us two ears, but only one mouth. This doesn't mean that we shouldn't express our needs, requests, and desires to God. We should. But it does mean that we shouldn't allow what *we* have to say keep us from hearing what *He* wants to say.

A SAINT SPEAKS: *"Note well, that we must hear Jesus speak if we expect Him to hear us speak. If we have no ear for Christ, He will have no ear for us."*

—CHARLES H. SPURGEON

Deliberately listening for God's voice seems to be a lost art. Perhaps we don't really believe He will respond to something so ordinary and straightforward. Instead we try to get God's attention by engaging in more activity. We even think that He won't be pleased with us if we aren't busy doing something for Him. But we don't release the power that sustains the Christian walk if we are so busy—even in religious activity—that we don't take time to hear Him. God wants us to seek His direction first. And that means carving out some time for stillness. We allow the Enemy to win a victory every time we let interruptions keep us from listening to God.

I begin my quiet time, but then the phone rings and I answer. Satan cheers.

I wait until the end of the day to listen to God, but then find myself too tired to stretch my spiritual earlobes. Satan applauds.

In the stillness of the morning, I lean my elbows on heaven's windowsill to commune with the Lord, but then I decide to read my e-mail first. Satan laughs.

Satan is thrilled with every new satellite TV option, magazine subscription, Internet group, and cell phone upgrade. Each "improvement" plunges us farther into the abyss of busyness that makes God's voice sound like a distant echo. Busyness turns our prayers into mindless requests and meaningless babble.

A SAINT SPEAKS: *"O God, give me grace today to recognize the stirrings of Thy Spirit within my soul and to listen most attentively to all that Thou has to say to me. Let not the noises of the world ever so confuse me that I cannot hear Thee speak."*

—JOHN BAILLIE

Carving out time in our day to purposefully listen for God's voice plugs us in so we can hear the Spirit whisper. Listening to Him is how His ways come to light and our understanding grows. When we take time to intentionally tune in, we will hear the living Word minister to us individually and personally. It's a sure thing: If you listen, you will hear the voice that speaks eternally.

> **HE SPEAKS:** *"Be sure to pay attention to what you hear. The more you do this, the more you will understand—and even more, besides. To those who are open to my teaching, more understanding will be given."*
>
> —MARK 4:24–25

Discipline Yourself to Listen

One evening after a speaking event, I was eagerly seeking the haven of my hotel room when one of the attendees cornered me in the lobby. She began to unravel a long story about what had brought her to this event. She was a sweet woman, but she was very talkative, and I was tired after the demanding day. I tried to be attentive, but my mind just wouldn't cooperate. I heard her, but I didn't really *hear* her. Don't get me wrong. I could have repeated everything she said, but nothing was really sinking in. I'm embarrassed to admit that my body was there, but my mind was already upstairs tucked in a warm bed.

God is more selective than that dear woman when it comes to speaking to someone. He wants to speak to those who *actively* listen. Unfortunately too often, we are *passively* listening. Passive listening is when we hear with our physical ears, but don't really attempt to digest or act upon the truth of what is being said. However, this kind of listening won't allow us to discern God's voice. That's because He isn't inclined to speak to someone whose body is there but whose interest is elsewhere.

God wants to speak to active listeners who look intently at God's Word and listen intently to what He has to say. In James 1:25, we are told, "But if you keep looking steadily into God's perfect law—the law that sets you free—and if you do what it says and don't forget what you heard, then God will bless you for doing it."

Jesus reminds us of this fifteen times in the New Testament by saying, "He who has ears to hear, let him hear!" The Greek word used for *hear* doesn't mean just to be endowed with the faculty of hearing. It means to understand the essence of what is being said.

Over the years I've often heard believers encouraging one another to "listen" for the voice of God. But for some reason it never occurred to me that this was a practical discipline I needed to exercise in my intimate time with Him. I believed that God wanted more out of my prayer life with Him, and so did I. However, it wasn't until I began to take seriously the art of listening and making prayer more about God and less about me that my prayer life began to change, and I began to hear from Him.

> **A SAINT SPEAKS:** *"First, it is 'me and Him.' I come to prayer conscious of myself, my need, my desires. I pour these out to God. My second prayer becomes 'Him and me.' Gradually, I become more conscious of the presence of God than of myself. Then it is only 'Him.' God's presence arrests me, captivates me, warms me, works on me."*
>
> —STEPHEN VERNEY

Active listening is a purposeful activity, and it takes work. If you want to become an active listener, you need to engage all the parts of your being—your body, soul, and spirit. You must control your body's urge to move around and your mind's urge to wander, so your spirit will be open and receptive to the Lord's voice.

If you are someone who enjoys activity as much as I do, this may be quite a challenge. I can honestly say that when I first began to make time to just be quiet and listen to Him, it was tough—until I started to hear Him, that is! Hearing the voice of the Almighty speak to me intimately changed my humdrum Christian experience from a discipline to a passion. Now I no longer study the Bible just as an instructional and theological tool. I read it as if it's God's love letter to me. I eagerly look into its pages as I sit still before God and listen for His voice.

I am in no way implying that it isn't possible to hear God amidst the regular activities of life. To the contrary, it's possible to hear God everywhere and in everything. But to reach that point, we must first purposefully discipline ourselves to be still and listen, so we learn to recognize His voice when He speaks.

There's no formula to follow to accomplish this. Your relationship with the Lord is personal, and He wants to deal with you as an individual. Just as intimacy between a husband and wife doesn't need to be prescribed at a detailed level, neither does your intimate time with the Lord. The experience will be different for everyone.

Nevertheless, there are three activities that stand out in the lives of believers who seek to engage in sincere fellowship with God: prayer, meditation on His Word, and worship. When you do these three things regularly, you create an atmosphere in which you can learn to recognize God's voice.

> **A SAINT SPEAKS:** *"We can make our heart a chapel where we can go anytime to talk to God privately. These conversations can be so loving and gentle, and anyone can have them."*
>
> —BROTHER LAWRENCE

Prayer

In talking about his prayer life, the apostle Paul said that he prays with mind and his spirit (see 1 Corinthians 14:15). My own prayer life used to be pretty much limited to mental prayer, and that kept me from experiencing the fullness of what prayer should be. Now during my prayer time, I begin by working through a mental list of things I know I need to bring to God's attention—things like confessing sins, thanking Him for specific things, expressing my needs and desires, and interceding for others. But when my mental list is complete, instead of ending my prayer time, I wait and quiet my mind so that I can pray with my spirit.

I turn my thoughts inward and allow the Holy Spirit to lead by bringing people or situations to mind that I wouldn't normally think of. When He causes me to recall sins I had forgotten or didn't realize I had committed, I immediately offer all of them to God in prayer, so the blood of Christ can cleanse me. When He brings a verse of Scripture to my mind, I find the passage in the Bible and meditate on its principles. Often the Holy Spirit leads me to worship God for one of His specific attributes.

There is a very distinct connection between Spirit-led prayer and discerning God's voice, for only the Spirit knows what God wants to say to us and only He can communicate it to us in a way we will understand. In this time of praying in the spirit, I trust the Spirit to direct my prayer time and move me toward a time of meditation on God and His Word.

> **A SAINT SPEAKS:** *"Meditation is the activity of calling to mind, and thinking over, and dwelling on, and applying to oneself, the various things one knows about the works and ways and purpose and promises of God."*
>
> —J. I. Packer

Meditation

Over and over again Scripture encourages believers to meditate on God and His Word. As I have taken this directive more seriously, I have discovered that some of the most precious times I have with God come not during a corporate worship experience but during a time of personal meditation. During this time in my secret place with God, I just sit silently in His presence, sometimes with a specific Bible verse on my mind.

Since this kind of meditation involves slowly dissecting the Word of God, I may contemplate only one verse during my time with Him. When I slowly and deliberately allow the words of a passage to wash over me, I inevitably sense the Lord speaking to me.

HE SPEAKS: *"I honor and love your commands. I meditate on your principles."*

—PSALM 119:48

As I meditate on a verse, I will often insert my name or a personal pronoun into it to make it more personal. If I'm reading and meditating on a Bible story, I will become the main character so that it's not merely someone else's experience with God but my own. I ask myself what God would have me do as a result of what I have contemplated.

My Bible and journal are my only companions during this time. I write the thoughts that the Spirit brings to my mind and record the messages I sense the Lord is giving me through the passage I've chosen to contemplate. I find that the thoughts I journal will often answer these questions:

- What does it reveal to me about God?

- What spiritual principle does it teach?

- Am I living in a way that is contrary to its truth?

- How does it relate to my current circumstances?

- How should I respond as a result of what I have read and contemplated?

Meditation is a discipline because it requires you to control your desire to fill in the silence with activity. It means that you just "waste time" pondering Scripture, God's goodness to you, and the goodness of God Himself. Meditation almost always leads to spontaneous worship of God.

A SAINT SPEAKS: *"I close my eyes to shut out visual stimuli. . . . I close my ears by dealing authoritatively with distractions that threaten my ability to tune in to God. I close a series of shutters on the surface level of my life, thus holding at bay hindrances to hearing the still small voice of*

God, and I release a trigger that gives deeper, inner, hidden parts of myself permission to spark to life."

—JOYCE HUGGETT

Worship

Sometimes I use praise and worship music as the backdrop to my time with God. While alone at my kitchen table or in my bedroom, I wait for Him with my spiritual ears attuned to what He wants to say to me. I ponder the lyrics and allow them to guide me as to how I should worship God during this time with Him.

As I pray, I am often moved to get down on my knees or lie prostrate on the floor in a position of surrender and humility. As the music envelops me, the awareness of His presence overwhelms and encourages me. My heart burns within me as I sit with Him and wait for Him to speak. The Lord now has the chance to take the initiative because I have invited Him to. I sense His nearness and guidance. The words of the passage I'm meditating on come alive and words of thanksgiving and praise erupt from within me.

In sharing with you the details of my typical prayer time, my hope is not that you will copy me, but that it will motivate you to spend personal time with God. Remember, He longs for intimacy with you. Matthew 6:6 promises that He is in the secret place waiting to spend time with you. It's a priority on His list, and it should be a priority on yours as well. My friend, *make* time to spend with Him. He is waiting to speak to anyone who will listen.

Ask the Lord to heighten your senses so that your spiritual ears are tuned in. He can and will give you an awareness of His presence, His activity, and His voice in all the activities of your life. Is your heart tuned in? Are your ears wide open?

HOW DO YOU KNOW IT'S GOD'S VOICE?

"I know the Lord is speaking to me when He gives me wisdom to solve the many problems that I encounter on a daily basis. I know the Lord is speaking to me when He shows me the ways of peace amid great turmoil around me. I know the Lord is speaking to me when He repeats the same message through many different venues in a short period of time. Lastly, I know the Lord is speaking to me whenever I am willing to stop and listen."

—BEN CARSON

PART : TWO

Communicating with God Today

"Behold, the Lord our God has shown us His glory

and His greatness, and we have heard His voice . . .

we have seen today that God speaks with man."

—DEUTERONOMY 5:24 (NASB)

"God speaks with man . . ." In every age and every culture, people desire to commune with God. Often unaware of the reason for their longing, their searching soul seeks direction from extraneous sources only to be left with a bigger emptiness. Connection with the one true God is the only thing that can fill the "God-size" hole in the human spirit. To satisfy this need, the Almighty has continually sought an appropriate way to fellowship with His people in each generation. In Old Testament times, His voice was primarily heard through miraculous signs. In the Gospels, He spoke through His Son. Today, in His sovereignty, He has chosen His precious indwelling Spirit to be the clearest way to address the people of this age.

But regardless of the method He chooses to use, one thing has not changed: He is still speaking today! And His voice is no less discernable than in biblical times.

The Lord delights in us, and He longs to spend time with us. He has words of infinite wisdom and personal guidance that He is eager to share. He is always there waiting, in the secret place, to listen, offer comfort, peace, hope, and direction. For all who belong to Him and long to know His will, God invites us to draw near, so He can speak to us.

A Saint Speaks

"Far be it from me to deny that spectacular experiences occur or that they are, sometimes at least, given by God. But . . . the still small voice—or the interior or inner voice, as it is also called—is the preferred and most valuable form of individualized communication for God's purposes."

—DALLAS WILLARD

3

A Marvelous Voice

"God's voice thunders in marvelous
ways; he does great things beyond
our understanding."

—JOB 37:5 (NIV)

*God, if You want me to marry him, let me know by having him
ask me to the office party.*

*Lord, if I'm supposed to take that job, reveal Your will by having
them offer me more money.*

*Father, if this is the house I'm supposed to buy, show me by giving
me the down payment by tomorrow.*

The list goes on and on, doesn't it? I'm sure you could come
up with your own list of divine demands that you have proposed to God. Your list would probably look different than
mine, but our goal would be the same. We want God to show
us His will in a tangible way—a sensational way. We want
something that will appeal to one of our five senses.

What we want is for God to speak today the same way He
spoke in Old Testament times. It seemed much easier to discern God's voice back then. Why, you may ask, doesn't God
speak to me as He did in that early age? I struggled with that

question too. When I read the miraculous ways that God often chose to lead the Israelites, I found it easy to envy them. When I've needed to make a decision, how I've often wished that the cloud that led them by day would appear! In fact, I would often pray for a sensational sign. I wanted to physically hear, see, or feel something. That seemed to me to be the clearest way to discern God's voice. I wanted a concrete way to know for sure that God was the one speaking.

I can recall trying to discern God's leading about a singing career, by asking Him to have a certain phone call come by a certain time. Not only did the call not come at that time; it never came at all!

Perhaps, like me, you've discovered that we can't always depend on external means to discover God's will. Although on occasions, God has honored my request for a miraculous sign, it hasn't been my normal experience to hear from Him in sensational ways. I suspect that might be true of you as well. Now I realize why: that isn't the main way He speaks to believers today.

> **A SAINT SPEAKS:** *"We pray for the manifestation of the glory of God in our midst along with an ever-increasing openness in us to the manner in which You choose to manifest that glory."*
>
> —R. T. KENDALL

A Constant Purpose

In seeking to understand the reasons why God spoke differently in the past than He does in the present, I began by studying Scripture. I was amazed at how many ways God has chosen to speak to His people. He spoke through:

- a burning bush (Exodus 3:4) and burning hearts (Luke 24:32)

- His glory (Numbers 14:22) and His humiliation (Philippians 2:8)

- a fire (Deuteronomy 5:24) and a cloud (Matthew 17:5)

- His name (Joshua 9:9) and His creation (Romans 1:20)

- visible signs (Judges 6:40) and an invisible Spirit (Matthew 10:20)

- visions (Psalm 89:19) and dreams (Matthew 2:12)

- teachers (Ecclesiastes 1:1) and evangelists (Acts 8:35)

- angels (Daniel 8:15) and apostles (2 Peter 3:2)

These are just a few of the many marvelous ways the Old and New Testaments say that God has spoken. In some cases, the Bible doesn't tell us how He chose to speak. We know only that "the Lord spoke" and that those who heard Him weren't in any doubt about who had spoken or what His message was. Whether He spoke to reveal His character or to give direction, God's voice was clear. From the very beginning of time, He has always spoken in ways that could be clearly understood because He wants us to recognize His voice. Though the method of delivery has changed, His purpose has remained the same.

> **HE SPEAKS**: *"The heavens tell of the glory of God. The skies display his marvelous craftsmanship. Day after day they continue to speak; night after night they make him known. They speak without a sound or a word; their voice is silent in the skies; yet their message has gone out to all the earth, and their words to all the world."*
>
> —Psalm 19:1–4

Come, take a little journey through time with me. I want to show you something.

A Changing Means

The primary way God spoke to His people as a whole in Old Testament times was through the *person of a prophet,* while the main way they could confirm the prophet's message was through *a visible sign.* Prophecy and signs went hand in hand.

When God wanted to warn His people about worshiping false gods, He had Elijah speak to them on Mount Carmel (1 Kings 18). First the prophet challenged them to make up their minds if they were going to serve God or Baal. When the people said nothing, Elijah proposed a contest. The prophets of Baal would choose two bulls. They would lay one on their altar and call on the name of their god; Elijah would lay the other on God's altar and call on the name of the Lord. Whichever one answered by setting fire to the wood would be the true God.

The priests of Baal went first. Despite their frantic efforts to get their god to respond, nothing happened. But when Elijah walked up to the altar and prayed, the fire of God immediately flashed down from heaven and burned up the offering. "When the people saw it, they fell on their faces and cried out, 'The Lord is God! The Lord is God!'" (1 Kings 18:39). Elijah first gave the people God's message, and then God gave a visible sign that confirmed the prophet's word.

> **HE SPEAKS:** *"Long ago God spoke many times and in many ways to our ancestors through the prophets. But now in these final days, he has spoken to us through his Son. . . . The Son reflects God's own glory, and everything about him represents God exactly."*
>
> —HEBREWS 1:1–3

When Christ came, things changed. The Son was the Father's message to all mankind—a complete revelation of who He is and what His purposes are. The primary way God spoke to His people when Jesus walked on earth was *through the person of His Son.* Christ, in turn, confirmed God's word through *miracles.* Christ and His miracles worked hand in hand.

The most important message that God sent mankind through His Son is found in John 3:16, "God so loved the world that he gave his only Son, so that everyone who believes in him will not perish but have eternal life." In order that people would believe this message, Jesus confirmed it through miracles.

In John 11, we learn that after hearing that His friend Lazarus was critically ill, Jesus deliberately waited two days before He went to see him. By the time He arrived, Lazarus had been in the tomb for four days. When Lazarus's sister Martha greeted Jesus, she said, "Lord, if you had been here, my brother would not have died" (v. 21).

Jesus responded, "I am the resurrection and the life. Those who believe in me, even though they die like everyone else, will live again. They are given eternal life for believing in me and will never perish" (vv. 25–26). Jesus then confirmed that this message was from God by raising Lazarus from the dead.

As Jesus approached the time of His own death, He told His disciples that He was about to leave this world and go to the Father. "It is actually best for you that I go away," He said, "because if I don't, the Counselor won't come. If I do go away, he will come because I will send him to you" (John 16:7). The Counselor arrived on Pentecost, when God sent the Holy Spirit to dwell in His followers. With this, God initiated the primary way He still speaks to us today.

In Old Testament times, the Holy Spirit wasn't a permanent part of the lives of everyone who believed in Yahweh. He only came to specific people at a specific time in order to achieve a specific task. When that task was accomplished (or when those people sinned or rebelled), the Holy Spirit withdrew. But after Jesus ascended to the Father, the Holy Spirit became a permanent fixture in the lives of believers. Ever since then, the Spirit has revealed the mind of God individually and continually to every saint.

Just before He ascended to heaven, Jesus told His disciples what He wanted them to do: "Go into all the world and preach the good news to all creation" (Mark 16:15 NIV). They were to spread God's spoken word, so that those who heard it might believe it. Jesus gave them the power to confirm it through miracles. "Then the disciples went out and preached everywhere, and the Lord worked with them and confirmed his word by the signs that accompanied it" (v. 20 NIV).

The reason the apostles and their close associates performed miracles was the same reason that Jesus had performed them—to confirm His spoken words. Once the words were written down, there was no longer a need to rely on miracles to confirm the truth of God's message. This doesn't mean that God doesn't still perform miracles. It just means that we don't have to depend on them to know when God is speaking.

Over time, Christians divinely inspired by the Holy Spirit, came to agree on which writings belonged in the New Testament. Since then, the primary way God has spoken to His people has been *through the person of the Holy Spirit,* who confirms God's *written Word* and applies it to our life. The Holy Spirit and the Bible go hand in hand.

> **A SAINT SPEAKS:** *"When God speaks, He does not give revelation about Himself that contradicts what He has already revealed in Scripture. Rather, God speaks to give application of His Word to specific circumstances in your life. When God speaks to you. . . . He is applying to your life what He already says in His Word."*
>
> —RICHARD BLACKABY

A Changeless Canon

To say that God doesn't speak to us today primarily in sensational ways (ways that appeal to the senses) isn't to say He can't do so. As believers we must always leave room for God to be God, and that means remaining open to the possibility of the miraculous.

God alone chooses how to speak to us. The same God who chose to speak audibly through a donkey to Balaam is the same God we desire to hear from today (Numbers 22). Who are we to say that He cannot or will not do it again? I know some very godly people who have heard from

God in ways that a lot of us would consider unorthodox, yet I don't discount the sincerity of their encounter with God. We must be willing to put aside our preconceived notions about how God speaks so that we can hear the Spirit's voice.

Having said this, I must also say that even if God chooses to speak in miraculous ways today, these ways do not lay the *foundation* for us to hear from Him. Rather, they just provide *confirmation* of the messages we receive through the Holy Spirit's leading and the guidelines of Scripture.

A couple of years ago, I sensed for several weeks that the Lord wanted me to take a new direction spiritually and personally. I had to make some decisions that I knew were going to stretch my faith and challenge me in many ways. I was hesitant to make them because I was a little fearful about moving forward in the direction I felt the Lord was leading. It would have been far more comfortable for me to stay where I was and cling to what God had already established. Yet in my prayer time and Bible study, I sensed the Holy Spirit asking me to move forward.

During that time, I attended a brand-new Bible study. I didn't know anyone in the group, and no one knew me. At the end of the message, the teacher, a very godly person whose relationship with the Lord I respected, spoke to me with words that were unmistakably straight from God.

"I'm sorry I don't know your name," he said, "but I just feel prompted to share something with you. I began to pray for you when you came into the Bible study today. For some reason, the Lord gave me a mental picture of an old rickety train track. All of a sudden a futuristic streamlined train roared down the tracks. This train was like nothing I had ever seen before.

"Young lady, I believe the Lord wants to do something new in your life. What He has accomplished in your life so far has been extraordinary, but He doesn't want you to cling to it. The old framework of His past work just provides the track for His upcoming work. He has something new—something like you've never seen before—for you, your family, and your ministry."

With that, he opened his Bible to Isaiah 43:18–19 (THE MESSAGE) and read, "Forget about what's happened; don't keep going over old history. Be alert; be present. I'm about to do something brand-new. It's bursting out! Don't you see it? There it is!"

> **HE SPEAKS:** *"When the Spirit of truth comes, he will guide you into all truth. He will not be presenting his own ideas; he will be telling you what he has heard."*

—JOHN 16:13

This message shook me to my core, for it confirmed what the Holy Spirit had already been telling me. To be honest, I didn't know what to do with this. Hearing from God in this way seemed a little unconventional to me. But I couldn't deny the relevance of what the Bible teacher had said. I knew God was speaking, so I chose to obey. Since then it has become very clear that the words of a fellow believer had confirmed externally what I had already heard internally from God.

A word of caution is needed here, however. I believe that the gift of prophecy is a very real gift that the Spirit gives to New Testament believers as He wills (1 Corinthians 12:10). By this, I mean that God gives some believers a divine ability to share a message *from Scripture* that applies to a person's life and confirms His leading in specific situations. However, I do *not* believe that messages that either add to or take away from the Scriptures are messages from God. The Bible is the standard against which to measure anything you hear from God by other means. Anything the Holy Spirit reveals to you will *always* match up with the written Word. Why? Because the Holy Spirit was the One who gave us the Scriptures in the first place (2 Timothy 3:16), and He will never contradict Himself. There are no exceptions to this rule. You might feel very strongly that God has spoken to you about a particular subject. But if what you heard contradicts Scripture in any way, it isn't a message from God.

God is no longer in the business of revealing new doctrine. The canon of Scripture is closed. Everything that God seeks to reveal about Himself and His purposes can be found in the complete and comprehensive revelation of Scripture.

A SAINT SPEAKS: *"Listening to God today is not about newness but about 'nowness.'"*

—JOYCE HUGGETT

This doesn't mean that God has lost His desire to speak to you personally. What it means is that He does so by applying the revealed Word to your specific situation. The Holy Spirit doesn't reveal new things; He illumines old things and applies the message to your life.

A Privileged People

It can be easy for us to hope that God will speak to us in a sensational way. But if we do, the Enemy can deceive us into thinking that the primary means by which we hear from God today isn't as significant or as powerful as the means He used in days of old.

While we often wish that we had what the Old Testament believers had, I think they probably would have wanted what we have—personal access to the voice of God. Old Testament believers had to rely on prophets and visible signs to discern God's voice, because the Scriptures weren't yet complete, and they didn't have continuous access to the Holy Spirit. We have what they never could have hoped for—direct contact with God Himself. This is the primary way God wants to lead His children now, and we should rely on it

If we seek to hear from God in sensational ways, we will miss out on the most personal means of communication possible with our great God. The most spectacular way God has ever spoken to His people is occurring right now—through the indwelling presence of the Holy Spirit. God saved the most intimate and marvelous means of communication just for us!

Now, instead of wishing that God would *do something* to reveal His will for me, I celebrate the fact that He has already done something by giving me the most precious gift of all through which to communicate. He has given me Himself in the person of the Holy Spirit. What could be better than that?

I hope that you will open your heart completely to what the Spirit wants to teach you and the *way* He wants to teach it to you. Ask the Lord to remove any barriers or preconceived ideas about how God communicates, so that you can really start to discern His voice.

HOW DO YOU KNOW IT'S GOD'S VOICE?

"I know the Lord is speaking to me when I stop listening to sounds from the world that feed my sense of pride and ambition. Instead, I fall quiet, tune in to God's great world around me, and actively listen. Sometimes nature speaks, telling me of God's majesty and glory. Sometimes God's Word speaks, reminding me of what God wants me to know. And sometimes the Spirit speaks, awakening my conscience, reminding me of failures, stirring my compassion and sense of justice, aligning me with God's will. I cannot control the voice of God or how it comes. I can only control my 'ears'—my readiness to listen and quickness to respond."

—PHILIP YANCEY

4

A Guiding Voice

> "Only those people who are led by
> God's Spirit are his children."
>
> —ROMANS 8:14 (CEV)

I was reading a good book and enjoying the smooth ride when suddenly our plane seemed to drop out of the sky. Some passengers screamed; some fell to the floor; some did both. The overhead compartments fell open and bags flew across the aisles. After what seemed like an eternity, the plane stabilized and the pilot came on the intercom to explain what had happened. The control tower at our destination had radioed the pilot to tell him that we needed to change altitude immediately, in order to avoid colliding with another plane. If the pilot hadn't listened and obeyed, there would have been a major disaster.

With all the navigational tools at their disposal, the people at the control center could see what the pilot couldn't. Their ability to see the whole picture, and the pilot's willingness to trust their guidance may have caused us a little turmoil, but it saved a lot of lives.

The Holy Spirit is to us what the control tower is to the airplane pilot: a guide who can see what we cannot. He seeks to guide us through this life in order to get us to the Father's desired destination for us. He sees the whole picture and knows when there's choppy weather or even a major disaster ahead. Any smart pilot will not try to navigate his own course without the help of someone who is able to see more than he can. If he were to do so, he would put his life and the lives of his crew and passengers in great danger. Likewise, if we don't have the Holy Spirit dwelling within us, we will not be connected with the Source of information that can steer us accurately. To hear God's voice and be guided into His will for you, you must have the Holy Spirit.

> **GOD SPEAKS:** *"You are controlled by the Spirit if you have the Spirit of God living in you. (And remember that those who do not have the Spirit of Christ living in them are not Christians at all.)"*

—ROMANS 8:9

Come In, Please!

The Holy Spirit is a person—the third member of the Trinity—and He is the primary way that God speaks personally to believers today. Receiving Him is an event that takes place at salvation, and having Him dwell in us is proof that we've entered a relationship with the Father. The Holy Spirit enters our life only by invitation, and you must personally extend that invitation to Him. No one can do it for you. You do this simply by placing *faith* alone in *Christ* alone for the remission of your sins.

When you do that, the Spirit of God immediately takes up residence in you. If you are a Christian, you aren't waiting for more of the Holy Spirit, or for the anointing of the Holy Spirit. Paul told the believers at Ephesus that when they *believed,* they immediately *received* (Ephesians 1:13). John reiterated this point: "The anointing which you have received from Him abides in you" (1 John 2:27 NKJV). If you're a believer, you received *all* of the Holy Spirit at the moment you accepted Christ as your Savior and Lord, and you *are* anointed.

Believers, tuck this truth deep into a corner of your heart: God has already given you everything pertaining to life and godliness (2 Peter 1:3). God doesn't give the Holy Spirit in installment plans or on layaway. You have all of Him right now!

The question is, "Have you ever invited Him in?" Scripture tells us that God reveals the personal truths we hunger for only to those who have the Holy Spirit. General revelation about the attributes of God are continually revealed to everyone through His creation (Romans 1:20), but He reveals deeper spiritual truths only to those who are in His family. People who haven't received the Holy Spirit can't understand these truths. It all sounds like foolishness to them, because only those who have the Spirit can understand what the Spirit means (1 Corinthians 2:14). Only believers are totally equipped to discern God's voice. And that process of hearing God begins with making sure that the Spirit does indeed live in you, so that you are equipped to hear Him clearly.

If you have placed your faith in Jesus Christ but are still struggling to discern His voice, please don't start to doubt your salvation. Remember learning to hear Him is a discipline that requires time spent in prayer, reading His Word, and meditating on it. Just as the more time we spend in any relationship yields better communication, we grow in our ability to hear God as we spend more time getting to know Him. But the process of hearing God begins by making sure that the Spirit does live in you, so that you are equipped to hear Him clearly.

Growing up, my parents did not choose to have cable television. But Jerry and I decided that we would like to have it for our new home. I will never forget the day the cable man arrived and installed the equipment. When he gave me a guided tour of my new television capabilities, I was amazed to discover there were hundreds of options. I couldn't believe that I had missed out on so much for so many years.

In the spiritual realm, there are a divine channels that are available to you. They have always been available, but only those who have the Spirit (through salvation) are able to tune in to these frequencies. When the Holy Spirit lives within you, you will be amazed as you recognize your potential to hear God

Let me show you how this works.

A SAINT SPEAKS: *"A continued guilty conscience following sincere repentance can be the Holy Spirit's way of telling us that we have not allowed or believed God to complete a desired work in us."*

—BETH MOORE

Transform Me!

All human beings are composed of three parts: body, soul, and spirit. Before salvation each of these is completely unregenerate (stubborn) and separated from God. There is no capacity to either commune with God or hear His voice.

Your body is the material part of you—what your friends see when they look at you. It allows you to have contact with the physical realm through your five senses.

Your invisible soul consists of your mind, will, and emotions. It makes you a unique individual with a distinct personality because it causes you to think, act, and feel differently from others.

Your spirit is the essence of who you are and allows you to have contact with the spiritual realm. It is this part of us that longs for a connection with a higher spiritual being. Many people seek to fill this void with options other than Jehovah God and find that they are left dissatisfied. That is because the human spirit was made for the Holy Spirit's presence. It is your human spirit that received the Holy Spirit when you became a believer. When He comes in, "the old life is gone. A new life has begun!" (2 Corinthians 5:17). Now your human spirit is no longer separated from God but is born again and regenerated. You can connect with the one true God.

When the Holy Spirit comes in, He immediately begins the process of renewing and transforming you, body and soul. The Spirit's desire is to sanctify us (2 Thessalonians 2:13) so that we begin to want what He wants, think what He thinks, and purpose to do His good pleasure. Understanding all of this is *essential* to understanding how to discern God's voice!

Because of the importance of this in understanding how God speaks to us, let's begin by examining how God speaks to us through the Holy Spirit.

Control Tower to Pilot!

Every human being has a deep inner voice called a conscience. This voice guides us and seeks to direct our choices. It's that little voice inside you that says you should or shouldn't do or say something. The problem with following your conscience is that it was developed and influenced by your life experiences, personal environment, traditions, and the truth or lies, to which it was exposed. Our conscience can be faulty. It can be seared by sin and even corrupted by others. So it is crucial to remember this important message: Our human conscience is *not* the voice of God. It isn't infallible. It can be "evil" (Hebrews 10:22), "defiled" (Titus 1:15), "weak" (1 Corinthians 8:7), or "dead" (1 Timothy 4:2).

My friend Rebecca was reared in a home in which all of the women were divorced. She was raised by a single mom who was also raised by a single mom. In their family, divorcing for trivial reasons and remarrying was the norm. As a result, Rebecca came to think that this was acceptable. Because of her family tradition, she found it easy to see divorce as the solution when she had problems in her own marriage.

After coming to know the Lord and receiving the Holy Spirit, Rebecca noticed a change in her feelings concerning her marriage. Before she was saved, her conscience would have allowed her to divorce her husband with no qualms. But now that she's under the influence of the Spirit and growing in the Lord, she feels conviction as the Holy Spirit begins to reprogram her conscience, to reflect His thoughts concerning her decisions. Her Spirit-led conscience now convicts her of the error of her traditional belief about divorce and encourages her to stick with her spouse through hard times.

Changing Frequency to the Divine Channel

When you become a Christian, your spirit becomes new. The Holy Spirit comes to dwell within you (Titus 3:5). Your conscience becomes awakened at salvation and gradually enlightened as it is continually cleansed by the Holy Spirit. As you cooperate, by surrendering your life and obeying His written Word, He begins to change your conscience. Instead of just assisting you in making moral decisions, your Holy Spirit-led conscience begins to discern between sin and righteousness, and it instructs you accordingly (John 16:8). This means that the same deep inner "knowing" that you had before salvation to steer your actions is the same one that can direct you now. But now, its communication with you will be different, because it has a different Guide.

> **A SAINT SPEAKS:** *"A seared conscience is the sinner's heritage. It is upon this that the Holy Spirit first lays His hand when He awakens the soul from its sleep of death. He touches the conscience and then the struggles of conviction come. He then pacifies it by the sprinkling of the blood, showing it Jesus and His cross. Then giving it the taste of forgiveness, it rests from all its tumults and fears"*
>
> —A. W. TOZER

Listen to the apostle Paul confirm the connection between the Holy Spirit with our human conscience.

- Romans 9:1—As he spoke to the Romans about his anguish over the Jews' rejection of the gospel, Paul said, "my conscience and the Holy Spirit confirm it."

- Acts 23:1 NASB—When Paul stood at a trial before Ananias the high priest and the Sanhedrian to defend his preaching, he

said, "Brethren, I have lived my life with a perfectly good conscience before God."

- 2 Timothy 1:3 NASB—As Paul set out to encourage young Timothy in ministry, he described his own ministry in this way, "I
  thank God, whom I serve with a clear conscience the way my
  forefathers did . . . "

In each case Paul is saying that his activities, no matter how different
from everyone else; his preaching, no matter how despised by the masses;
and his ministry, no matter how filled with persecution it may have been,
was all acceptable because there was an *agreement* that took place between
his conscience and the Holy Spirit. Paul says the Holy Spirit has confirmed
in his conscience that the direction he has chosen is in conjunction with
the will of God for him.

Your conscience is like the communication device the control tower used
to direct our pilot. It is the mechanism by which the Spirit works to give you
specific divine direction that will align you with His will and steer you away
from sin. He will give you the red light of conviction that means "stop"; the
green light of ease and peace that means "go"; or the yellow light of doubt
and uneasiness that means "wait." If you experience conviction in your life,
celebrate! That means the Holy Spirit is there. He's working, guiding, and
changing you! Even if His direction may sometimes be momentarily
uncomfortable, He can see the entire picture of your life and will save you
true disaster in the long run. He is steering you into God's will.

> **HE SPEAKS:** *"And we, who with unveiled faces all reflect*
> *the Lord's glory, are being transformed into his likeness with*
> *ever-increasing glory, which comes from the Lord, who is the*
> *Spirit."*
>
> —2 CORINTHIANS 3:18 (NIV)

Cynthia's conscience weighed on her heavily anytime she desired to
do anything that contradicted her strict upbringing. She had been taught

that it was wrong to do many things such as wearing pants or going to any type of movie. Her strict, legalistic background had formatted her conscience to bring guilt for almost everything she did.

Then she met the Savior and the Holy Spirit took up residence in her. As she saturated herself in the Word of God, the Spirit has reprogrammed her conscience. By confirming her Spirit-led conscience with God's Word, she now has peace to enjoy many of the freedoms that God has given her.

The Spirit has our best interest in mind. Many times I've made decisions that have gone against the prompting of the Holy Spirit because, even though I couldn't see the whole picture, I thought I knew best. But anytime I've done this, the results have been disastrous. Whether it was wearing a particular outfit that made "something inside me" feel uncomfortable or accepting an invitation to participate in something that I "just knew" I shouldn't, such experiences have made it easy for me to see how going with my Spirit-led conscience leads to outcomes that please the Lord and work together for my ultimate good.

> **A SAINT SPEAKS**: *"The Greek word for 'conscience' is found more than thirty times in the New Testament. It is* suneidesis, *which also literally means 'co-knowledge.' Conscience is knowledge together with oneself; that is, conscience knows our inner motives and true thoughts."*
>
> —JOHN MACARTHUR

Copy That

It is imperative that we remember that the change in our conscience is *gradual*. Our mind, will, emotions, conscience, and body will not be perfected until we see Him face-to-face in eternity. So as you listen to your Spirit-led conscience, we must *always* confirm what we hear.

God has chosen the Holy Spirit as the primary means to speak to His people in this generation because He *wants* us to discern His voice.

Therefore, He will graciously confirm what He is saying to us. I believe
He will do this in the small details of life, as well as the major decisions
we have to make. But as we are being transformed by the renewing of
our minds (Romans 12:2), here are some guidelines we can follow. These
will help us be certain we are hearing our Spirit-led conscience accurately.
I refer to these as the five M's of correctly hearing God.

1. *Look for the MESSAGE of the Spirit. Take time listening and paying close
   attention:* Earnestly seek God and turn your attention inward to
   see if what you are sensing carries the full weight of God and not
   the faulty values of your traditions and human conscience.
2. *Search the MODEL of Scripture for guidance:* If what you are hearing contradicts the whole counsel of God, as revealed in Scriptures or the character of God in any way, the message isn't from
   Him. In addition, keep your eyes open for the moment when Scripture *grips* you, speaking to a particular circumstance in your life.
3. *Live in the MODE of prayer. Take the matter to the Lord in prayer:*
   Direct what you are hearing back to God. If an issue is troubling
   you, don't spend time and energy worrying; use it to turn the matter
   back to God in prayer.
4. *Submit to the MINISTRY of Eli. Seek the counsel of a mature believer:*
   Choose a wise, mature believer who can discern God's leading in
   his or her own life. Then seek their counsel. But do this only after
   having first asked God.
5. *Expect the MERCY of confirmation. Look for God's use of circumstances,
   Scripture, and other believers to confirm His direction for your life:*
   God desires for us to know His will. Ask the Lord to confirm what
   you feel the Spirit is saying to you.

> **A SAINT SPEAKS:** *"God makes His desires known to those
> who stop at His Word, look in with a sensitive spirit, and
> listen to others. When we go to His Word, we stop long
> enough to hear from above. When we look, we examine our
> surrounding circumstances in light of what He is saying to
> our inner spirit (perhaps we prefer to call this our*

conscience). And when we listen to others, we seek counsel of wise, qualified people."

—CHARLES SWINDOLL

As you seek to get clarity on God's leading for you, be faithful to confess any sin He reveals so that the blood of Christ can cleanse it. This will keep your conscience in constant agreement with the Holy Spirit.

If you are listening for God's voice in your life, what words are resonating deep within you? What promptings do you recognize? If a voice seems strange, or in any way out of line with Scripture, assume that your uncertainty is the Holy Spirit's way of detecting a stranger's voice. Trust that the Holy Spirit's guiding voice will lead you into His will.

HOW DO YOU KNOW IT'S GOD'S VOICE?

"I know the Lord is speaking to me when I remember that the sheep recognize the Shepherd's voice, but not the Stranger's. I believe that if I'm in the Word, submitted to the Lord, walking in the Spirit, accountable to godly counsel, and paying attention to what God is up to in my circumstances, I can count on having the mind of Christ to guide me. On the other hand, if I feel unsure, rushed, afraid, or hesitant about a decision, it's probably because I'm hearing the Stranger's voice."

—LISA WHELCHEL

5

A Verifiable Voice

"The word of God is living and powerful, and sharper than any two-edged sword, piercing even to the division of soul and spirit, and of joints and marrow, and is a discerner of the thoughts and intents of the heart."

—HEBREWS 4:12 (NKJV)

I love to give gifts. I truly enjoy seeing people's faces light up when they open gifts I've picked out especially for them. Recently, it occurred to me that it would be neat to buy small gifts for a group of friends. I really thought it would be a great way to bring a ray of sunlight into the lives of these women.

Soon after I made that decision, my personal Bible study included Matthew 6:3–4, "When you give to someone, don't tell your left hand what your right hand is doing. Give your gifts in secret, and your Father, who knows all secrets, will reward you." I had read this passage many times, but now the sharp sword of the Spirit jumped off the page and pierced my soul.

When I thought about my gift idea in the light of this verse, I began to ask myself why I wanted to do this. What was my motive? Was I really doing it because I just wanted to do something nice for these women? Or did I want to impress them and draw attention to myself? As I prayed about it, the Holy Spirit convicted me that my flesh wanted attention. At least on that occasion, my desire to give gifts was a way to take for myself the glory that belongs only to God.

Have you ever wondered how you can be certain that your desires aren't leading you in the wrong direction? It's really very simple. Get into the Word and expect the Holy Spirit to speak to you through it. Through Scripture, you can verify if your intentions are in line with His. While you're reading the Word, the Spirit will be reading you!

Discerning God's Voice through His Word

When I was in college, a young man asked me to marry him. We were good friends, shared many interests, and I was very attracted to him. The problem was that he wasn't a Christian. When he asked for my hand in marriage, I had a strong emotional desire to say yes. However, I knew that my desire wasn't coming from the Holy Spirit because it contradicted Scripture, which says, "Don't team up with those who are unbelievers" (2 Corinthians 6:14).

It's easy to discern God's voice on broad issues of principle like this one, and there are many other instances in which God speaks clearly like this. But when it comes to matters that are specific to us—like which believer to marry, which job to take, which ministry to support—we tend to stop thinking that Scripture has the answer. Most often, we begin to ask our friends for their opinion instead of trying to find an answer in God's Word.

> **A SAINT SPEAKS:** *"When you read your Bible, receive and savor it like a love letter from God to you. Remember, you're reading in order to meet Someone. Ponder what you have read, and apply it to your present circumstances. Let it go*

down into the core of your being. And as you read, expect
Him to commune with you."

—BRUCE WILKINSON

I was once on a committee with a woman whose views were so different than mine that we couldn't work together. I sought advice from everyone I knew, but nothing helped. The tension between us was so thick that everyone noticed it. I didn't realize that I hadn't even asked God about how to resolve this problem.

Thank God for His grace. One day I chose 1 Kings for my Bible study. The first verse I read said, "And Hiram and Solomon made a formal alliance of peace" (5:12). Since I wanted peace in that troublesome relationship, I immediately read backward to see how those men had achieved it. I found that Solomon, who was in the middle of building the temple, asked King Hiram to help by doing what he and his people did best— chopping down cedar trees in Lebanon. Hiram felt needed and appreciated, and peace was the result.

Armed with God's specific word for my situation, I walked confidently into the next committee meeting. I opened it by acknowledging this woman's strengths and assigning her a task that suited her talents. The result has been the same kind of peace that Solomon and Hiram experienced. God spoke to me through His Word, I obeyed, and blessing followed.

I have learned that if I take time to seriously read, contemplate, and meditate on Scriptures, the Holy Spirit will supernaturally illumine them to cause me to know what God wants me to do. If I'm in a situation that's particularly taxing and I'm not sure what to do, I begin my Bible reading with a prayer that clearly explains my need and asks the Holy Spirit to give me clear direction as a result of the time I spend in God's Word. He doesn't always respond as quickly as I would like, but He always honors such requests from His children, in His own timing.

When He does reveal His will, we want to be sure we are listening and focusing on hearing His voice. Turn up the volume in your spiritual ears to catch the moment when a passage captures your attention, in an almost shocking way, and immediately draws your thoughts to how it applies to a specific situation in your life. When this happens, the Holy Spirit has orchestrated it. God has spoken.

When a Scripture comes to mind "out of nowhere" that speaks to the specific problem I'm facing, I'm learning not to dismiss it as mere coincidence. Instead I trust that the Holy Spirit is at work in me to reveal more about God and what my actions should be. When I discern His direction, it is then my responsibility to immediately apply that verse to my life and obey.

If you are having trouble discerning God's voice, could one of the problems be that you know what you should do but still wrestle with being obedient? If so, know that you are not alone. All believers have this same struggle. Even the great and faithful saints of the Bible found difficulty in always doing what they knew was the right thing. Paul talks about his struggles in Romans 7:15–19:

> "I don't understand myself at all, for I really want to do what is right, but I don't do it. Instead, I do the very thing I hate. I know perfectly well that what I am doing is wrong, and my bad conscience shows that I agree that the law is good. But I can't help myself, because it is sin inside me that makes me do these evil things. I know I am rotten through and through so far as my old sinful nature is concerned. No matter which way I turn, I can't make myself do right. I want to, but I can't. When I want to do good, I don't. And when I try not to do wrong, I do it anyway."

Remember, your body, mind, will, and emotions will not be perfected until you see Christ in eternity. Until then there is often a gap between what the Spirit is leading us to do and what our bodies and souls want to do. So how do we deal with bodies and souls that often want to do the opposite of what God is asking? First, we realize that our body is a "tool to do what is right for the glory of God" (Romans 6:13). We consistently present those tools to God as instruments to be used for His purposes. Second, we saturate our minds with the living Word of God that can penetrate the depths of our souls and literally change the way we think, feel, and desire. Third, we can rest in the promise of Hebrews 8:10 and Philippians 2:13. In both instances, God promises His people that because of His new covenant with us, He will cause us "to will and to work for His good pleasure" (NASB). The Spirit's precious work in us causes us to desire what He desires, so that we want to do what He is asking.

All of Me

When I became pregnant with my first son, Jerry and I were thrilled and excited. I eagerly watched for changes in my body and welcomed the feeling of the new life growing within me. One change in my body, though, was less pleasing: developing a love affair with chocolate that has never gone away! Something happened around my eight month of pregnancy that completely changed my taste buds. Before that time, I had never particularly cared about chocolate. Now I can't get enough of it. The new life developing within me was changing my tastes in a surprising way.

When the new life of the Holy Spirit takes up residence in you, He begins to change your taste buds. Things that once were important to you begin to fade away and you begin to desire the things of God. Since this change is happening *progressively, not instantly,* our body and soul will still send us messages. Sometimes it's difficult to discern whether we are listening to the Spirit's voice or our own. To clearly distinguish God's voice, it is necessary to confirm what we hear through His Word in order to obey.

> **A SAINT SPEAKS:** *"We obey God so that we can cooperate with His work within us. Because He loves us, He wants us to be more like Him. So He is 'growing' us up in grace. . . . Obedience means that we are cooperating with the transformation process."*
>
> —LOIS EVANS

Disciplining Your Soul

The Holy Spirit is using the Word to gradually purify our soul (mind, will, and emotions) to make us want to do what pleases God and brings Him glory. Often the Spirit prompts you to do something you don't want to do, and it just doesn't sound like a reasonable idea or something you feel like doing, but if you stay in the Word, the Holy Spirit will bring us around to God's way of thinking.

My husband was very satisfied with his corporate job, but one day, out of the blue, he had a strange thought: *Quit your job and work full-time with Priscilla.* Jerry thought the idea was absurd. For years he had worked a normal eight-to-five job with good pay and benefits, and he was well on his way up the ladder of success at his company. Leaving all that for self-employment in a ministry really wasn't something he wanted to do.

As in Jerry's case, your soul can often be what keeps you from being receptive to the things of God. Your mind and emotions prevent you from hearing what God wants you to do and even causes you not to heed His direction.

God had put His thought in Jerry's mind, and over time, Jerry was surprised to find that as he spent time in the Word of God, his thoughts and feelings about his job were changing. He was shocked to discover that he was beginning to feel dissatisfied with a job he had enjoyed for many years. In fact, he started to think that it was absurd to stay at his old job when God was giving him an opportunity to work full-time for His kingdom. Now, four years later, he has no desire to return to the job he once loved so much.

A SAINT SPEAKS: *"He writes his laws on our hearts and on our minds so that our affection and our understanding embrace them and we are drawn to obey instead of being driven to it."*

—HANNAH WHITALL SMITH

The Holy Spirit is constantly at work sanctifying you and changing your personality to suit His design for you. The more you surrender to Him and are conformed to the image of Christ, the less of a gap there will be between what He wants and what you want.

The book of James tells us how we can get our souls in step with our new spirit. Though it's written to believers, the author gives us some startling instructions: "Get rid of all the filth and evil in your lives, and humbly accept the message God has planted in your hearts, for it is strong enough to save your souls (James 1:21).

This verse says that, while our spirit was reborn when we were saved, our soul still needs to be renewed. The Spirit is busy at work to make this happen, but we must cooperate with Him.

As you hear God speak through His Word, He will radically change you. This is one of the most incredibly supernatural things about our relationship with God: His Spirit makes us different so that we desire to do the things that are pleasing to Him. I am so grateful that we don't have to serve Him out of duty, but rather out of love.

Whether you feel anything happening or not, when you spend time in the Word, I guarantee that a massive renovation is underway. Your very soul is being renewed. More is happening beneath the surface than you could ever imagine!

God is also at work to help you surrender your body to Him. He truly does want all of you. When the Holy Spirit came to dwell in you, your body became God's temple (1 Corinthians 3:16). But even though this is true, your sinful flesh will fight you every step of the way.

Disciplining Your Body

Yesterday, after eating a delicious meal, I was offered a decadent piece of chocolate cake. My stomach was completely full but my mouth seemed determined to devour that velvety chocolate. Though my stomach said no, my mouth said yes. So I ate it and immediately regretted it.

The disparity between what my stomach wanted and what my mouth wanted is a clear example of the struggle that exists between the flesh and the Spirit. Something inside of us—the Holy Spirit—tries to tell us what is best for us and says no. But the taste buds of our flesh say yes. Galatians 5 says that there is a constant war that wages between these two.

Paul gives us the solution. In Romans 12:1, he tells us how to experience victory over our bodies as we seek to follow the leading of the Spirit. He says, "Give your bodies to God. Let them be a living and holy sacrifice—the kind he will accept."

Please notice that Paul doesn't say that you have to fight really hard to experience victory in this area. He just says to give your body to God. Through Jesus you have already been given victory as a gift (1 Corinthians 15:57). God is already at work. You just have to cooperate in the process by purposefully yielding your body to Him.

This is something only you can do. Believe that God has given you every part of your body, not so you can use it for your own gratification but so that you can use it as a "tool to do what is right for the glory of God" (Romans 6:13). Give Him your hands to do His work, your feet to walk His path, and your ears to hear Him speak.

An African missionary once told a group of people that each morning before he got up to serve God in ministry he would literally present himself to God. He would stretch out across his bed and picture the bed as an altar, on which he was the sacrifice. He started each day by saying, "Lord, this day, I present myself as a tool for You. Today, I am Your living sacrifice."

> **A SAINT SPEAKS:** *"I believe in the truth found in Romans 12:1–2. If I have presented my body to Him as a living sacrifice and I have, and I'm being transformed by the renewing of my mind then I'm able to prove—to put to the test—what His will is. He will show me that which is good, acceptable, and perfect for me."*
>
> —KAY ARTHUR

Devoting Yourself to God's Word

If you're serious about learning to discern God's voice, you must get serious about studying His Word. It has become almost cliché in Christian circles to encourage one another to have a "quiet time," but this is far more serious than you might think. The more we immerse ourselves in the Word, the more closely our thoughts, emotions, and decisions will align with what the Holy Spirit is saying to us.

Every day, from every conceivable source, we're saturated with messages that contradict God's truths. If we don't consciously attempt to combat those messages by saturating our minds with Scripture, our souls will be conformed to the world's standards instead of God's. The more Scripture you have hidden in your heart, the more opportunity the Holy Spirit will have to bring it instantly to your mind to verify how you should proceed.

> **HE SPEAKS:** *"I have hidden your word in my heart, that I might not sin against you."*
>
> —PSALM 119:11

Recently I spoke to a group of women about spending time in the Word of God on a regular basis. Afterward a woman came to me almost in tears because she was so discouraged. Besides being a wife and the mother of four children, she worked full-time. She believed it was impossible for her to spend enough time in God's Word to make a significant difference in her life. I could empathize with this woman, and you probably can too. Most of us feel we don't have enough time to meditate on Scripture. Let me tell you the same thing I told her.

If you find it difficult to set aside time to spend with God, here's a simple way to start. Select one verse each week and write it on two index cards. Stick one card to your bathroom mirror and the other to the steering wheel of your car or another place where you will see it frequently. Every day for seven days keep this verse in your heart and mind as you wash your face, brush your teeth, run errands, and do the mundane duties of your day.

All day long, meditate on it and ask the Lord to speak to you and teach you—whether you're at the park with your kids, sitting at your desk, peeling potatoes for dinner, or preparing for a committee meeting. Throughout the day ask Him to show you clearly how this verse applies to the situations you face. Keep a record of the times God uses that verse to give you direction in your daily life. By the end of the week, this verse will be inscribed on your heart, and you will see how God has used His living Word to speak to you personally.

Recently I have been studying the book of Job. Chapter 28 talks about seeking wisdom and verses 23–24 say, "God surely knows where it can be found, for he looks throughout the whole earth, under all the heavens." This is the verse that I currently have taped to my bathroom mirror. So when I was struggling to find a favorite photo album that had been missing for several weeks, the Holy Spirit caused me to think of these verses in light of my current dilemma. Instead of spending time looking again, I acknowledged the truth found in the verses and asked for God's help and wisdom. When I returned from running errands later in the afternoon, my scrapbook was sitting on my pillow! My husband had been moving furniture around and found it. God honored my decision to rely on the counsel of Scripture in a very surprising way that left an indelible mark on me. Now, when facing much bigger life issues, I think, "If God would respond to a small need like this one, then surely I can count on Him for these greater concerns as well."

An unbelievable excitement comes over me when I hear God's voice speaking to me clearly through His Word like this. When I hear, I know that God is inviting me to join Him in His purposes and supernatural activity. I'm continually in awe that this very old book can give me such clear instructions for the present. With all my heart, I wish I could sit down with you to share how relevant God's Word is to your life today.

If you truly want to know how to discern God's voice, you must verify whatever you think you hear from God in light of His written Word. The Bible isn't just an old book that has a lot of theology for us to digest; it's the living Word of God. When you read it, you should feel the warmth of God's breath on it as the Holy Spirit applies it to your particular situation, regardless of how specific and personal it is.

James is so sure of the power of God's Word to lead us to discern God's voice correctly that he tells us: "If you keep looking steadily into God's perfect law—the law that sets you free—and if you do what it says and don't forget what you heard, then God will bless you for doing it" (James 1:25). Think about it—a very old book giving specific, relevant direction meant to bless us today. Now *that's* spectacular!

HOW DO YOU KNOW IT'S GOD'S VOICE?

"I know that the Lord is speaking to me when I read, 'I will never forsake you' (Hebrews 13:5). The sentence falls like a hand on my shoulder. The Bible is to God what a surgical glove is to the surgeon. He reaches through it to touch deep within us. When anxiety termites away at peace, I read this passage: 'Do not be anxious about anything, but in everything, by prayer and petition, with thanksgiving, present your requests to God' (Philippians 4:6 NIV). The words stir a sigh from the soul. Let's try not to make a decision, whether large or small, without sitting before God with open Bible, open heart, open ears, imitating the prayer of Samuel: 'Your servant is listening' (1 Samuel 3:10).

—MAX LUCADO

6

A Persistent Voice

"God has spoken plainly, and I have heard it many times."

—PSALM 62:11

One day my neighbor knocked on my front door. I wasn't in the mood for company and not really dressed for visitors, so I stayed tucked away in my room and tried to ignore her. I thought that after a few unanswered knocks, she would go away. But she didn't. She kept right on banging on the door. The more I ignored her, the more she knocked. After several long minutes, I grudgingly answered the door.

Boy was I glad I did! She had come to tell me that she saw smoke coming from the side of my house. How thankful I was for her persistent attempts to speak to me!

When God has a message for us, He is also persistent. He doesn't just give you His message once and then go away, saying, "Oh well, I guess she's busy right now."

As you seek to hear God's voice in the specific situation you're facing right now, ask yourself these questions: "What persistent stirrings have I encountered? What do I sense God is asking me to do internally, and how is He corroborating that message externally?"

When God speaks to you within and confirms it without,

be on the lookout for His direction. If you notice a consistent message confirmed through the leading of the Holy Spirit, Scripture, circumstances, and other people, pay close attention. God is repeating Himself to make sure you get the message.

> **HE SPEAKS:** *"Look! Here I stand at the door and knock. If you hear me calling and open the door, I will come in, and we will share a meal as friends."*
>
> —REVELATION 3:20

God Keeps on Speaking

Revelation 3:20 is often used to refer to the Lord's desire to win those who don't yet believe in Him. Yet this passage was actually addressed to the early church in Laodicea. Its members were already believers, but their relationship with Christ was lukewarm. Although the Lord rebuked them for their halfhearted spirituality, He also told them that He was still pursuing them, still knocking at the door of their hearts, still desiring a more intimate relationship with them. He wanted more, and He was willing to keep on knocking until they opened the door and let Him in.

Throughout Scripture, we see God persistently calling out in an attempt to turn deafened ears and hardened hearts toward Him. He persistently pursues His saints, even when we are running in the opposite direction. Because He loves us, He persists. The Holy Spirit works in our hearts, in the hearts of others, and in the events of our lives to point us in His direction.

Job 33:15–21 gives just some of the many ways God spoke persistently in the Old Testament in His unrelenting attempts to cause them to hear and heed His voice.

- "He speaks in dreams, in visions of the night." (v. 15)

- "He whispers in their ear and terrifies them with his warning." (v. 16)

- "He causes them to change their minds; he keeps them from pride." (v. 17)

- "He keeps them from the grave, from crossing over the river of death." (v. 18)

- "God disciplines people with sickness and pain, with ceaseless aching in their bones." (v. 19)

- "They lose their appetite and do not care for even the most delicious food." (v. 20)

- "They waste away to skin and bones." (v. 21)

In each of these examples, the Lord arranges events so His people will realize that He is speaking to them.

Do you see? God doesn't just speak to His people once and then throw His hands in the air. He keeps at it. He orders our circumstances, so that they relentlessly bombard our thoughts and hearts with His message until we are convinced of its authenticity.

Aren't you thankful that God never gives up on you, even if it takes you a while to recognize that He is the One speaking? I'm so glad that God knows that we're just dust. He knows that as long as we're clothed in the flesh, we aren't always going to get it right; and when we do, it will have taken us many tries. But God uses each mistake to teach us a little more about how to recognize when He is speaking.

God Uses Circumstantial Evidence to Convict Us

Serendipity is the name of one of my favorite romance movies. In it, a series of fortuitous events bring a man and a woman together despite unbelievable odds. Everywhere they turn, events conspire to bring them face-to-face with their destiny—each other. Of course the movie ends, as all good romances should, by bringing the two together in blissful love.

The title of this movie has become synonymous with the word *fate*. It's now generally used to imply that the stars have aligned to influence events in order to point people in a certain direction. But while an unbeliever might attribute this to "karma" or "coincidence," a believer will attribute it to the Someone who lined up the stars in the first place.

Believers know and celebrate the fact that behind serendipity stands the sovereign One who seeks to speak to us and lead us in His ways. Persistent internal inklings matched by external confirmation are often the way God directs believers into His will. God is at work in our circumstances to point us in His direction.

Never think that the circumstances of your life have nothing to do with God's will! They have everything to do with it. When you're seeking God's guidance, you should always reflect on the events the Lord is allowing to occur in your life.

> **A SAINT SPEAKS:** *"I know that the Lord is speaking to me when He impresses something on my spirit internally and confirms it through a person or circumstance externally."*
>
> —TONY EVANS

About a year ago, a friend sent me a book about silent prayer. The book explains how purposeful periods of silent prayer can help believers hear God's voice. I was very drawn to the spiritual journey of the author, and I read the book twice. As my heart burned within me, I knew that the Lord was calling me to experience Him in prayer in a brand-new way.

Not long after I finished reading the book the first time, my personal Bible study led me to Ecclesiastes 5:1, "As you enter the house of God, keep your ears open and your mouth shut!"

It seemed as if somebody had sneaked a brand-new verse into the Bible! I didn't remember ever having seen it before. Now these words from the passage leapt off the page and gripped my heart. It confirmed the message of the book I had been so drawn to and what I sensed the Holy Spirit was leading me to do.

Several days later, I was in a meeting when one of the ladies seated around the table mentioned an upcoming retreat that some women in our church were going to take. When I asked about it, she told me that it was a silent prayer retreat. Women would gather to spend thirty-six hours of silence in anticipation of hearing the voice of God.

I was so shocked that I dropped the papers I was holding. Other than in the book I had just read, I had never heard of such a thing before that day. In fact, I was pretty sure that no one I knew would do anything as weird as what I was feeling compelled to do.

Within weeks, our office received a call from Fox Network. They were creating a program on contemplative prayer called "Be Still." They asked me to be a part of this project that was designed to help Americans see the importance of spending time in stillness before God. I knew immediately that God wanted me to be a part of this project. God was using the circumstances of my life to confirm the direction in which He was leading me personally and in ministry. I knew He was speaking directly to me.

Is this all mere coincidence? I think not! God orchestrates all these events, so He can meet us there and speak to us.

> **A SAINT SPEAKS:** *"When what I hear is confirmed by godly people in my life, I know the Lord is speaking to me. I also know He is speaking when what I hear and am led to do cannot be done without His assistance, protection, and guidance. He only speaks what brings glory to Himself!"*

—BISHOP KENNETH ULMER

God Speaks to Us Where We Are

It is simpler for us to believe that God is only orchestrating the good things in our lives, but Scripture is full of people whose most life-changing encounters with the Lord occurred while they were in places they didn't want to be:

- Moses was leading sheep in the middle of a dry desert. (Exodus 3:1)

- Daniel was in the lions' den. (Daniel 6:20)

- Jonah was in the whale's belly. (Jonah 2:1)

- John the Baptist was in prison. (Luke 3:20)

- Lazarus was in the grave. (John 11:17)

The same thing happens today. Even difficult life circumstances are being used to give us a clear reception to hear His voice. Recently, I was in a bad situation when I encountered God.

I was so glad to get an invitation to speak in Orlando, Florida, because it meant that my husband and I could bring our boys along and spend a couple of days at Disney World before the conference began. Once there, our boys were enjoying a small, closed-off area outfitted with slides, jungle gym equipment, and water features suited to small children. Children could explore these smaller theme parks to their hearts' content while parents could relax knowing there was only one way in and out.

While Jerry went to get us a snack, I relaxed on a bench in the Winnie the Pooh section and watched the boys run in and out of waterfalls and under huge tunnels. Jackson found the jungle gym on the far side of the park and quickly climbed up to slide down, giggling as he made his landing on the artificial grass. Again and again he climbed the side and slid down. After a while, Jerry Jr. spotted the fun, toddled over, and tried to make his way up the ladder.

I knew he couldn't do this safely on his own, but I didn't want him to miss out on the fun, so I left my spot, went around to the back of the jungle gym, and helped him climb up. I scaled the ladder with him and walked him across the bridge that led to the enclosed slide. I seated him on my lap, and we slid down together. He landed with a huge smile.

It only took a couple of minutes, and as soon as we finished sliding, I immediately looked around for Jackson. Figuring he was probably getting ready to slide down again, I looked back up at top of the jungle gym. He wasn't there. I checked the back of the jungle gym, but he wasn't there either. I called his name, but he didn't answer. I peered in the tunnels and under the waterfalls. No Jackson.

My heart began to beat a little faster as I scooped Jerry Jr. into my arms for safekeeping while I searched for Jackson. I ran to the back of the play park so I could see the entire area. I asked the other mothers sitting nearby if they had seen my son. They hadn't. One by one they kindly began to get up and help me search for him. Soon all of the parents in the area were looking for Jackson.

The Disney World attendant stationed at the area came over to help and asked me all the questions a mother never wants to be asked. "What does he have on? Where did you last see him? What name does he answer to?" With each question she asked, more and more panic set in. I broke down and sobbed uncontrollably. I can't describe the fear I felt. With each passing minute, I became more and more certain that I would never see my son again. I begged God with a passion I had never known to please bring Jackson back.

Fifteen minutes later, Jackson was found. When I had gone to help his brother, he had assumed that I had left the park and had gone to find me. Although he was now safe, the tears continued to stream down my face as I sat cuddling both of my children and thanking the Father for His mercy and protection.

Then the Lord spoke: *Priscilla, can you imagine what it was like for Me when I chose to separate Myself from My only Son for your sake?* No one can know the torment in the Father's heart when He "made Christ, who never sinned, to be the offering for our sin, so that we could be made right with God through Christ" (2 Corinthians 5:21). But right then, because of the awful separation I had endured and the crushing heartache I had experienced, I could at least imagine what it was like. I believe God allowed me to be in that dreadful situation so I would have a much deeper understanding of the depth of His love for me.

You aren't where you are today by chance. Sometimes God's voice is clearest when we are in circumstances we don't prefer. There's something in your current situation that God is going to use to draw you closer to Him so He can tell you something about Himself and His plan for your life. No matter what tight spot you may find yourself in, ask God to open your ears to what He is saying in your circumstances.

Are you in a job you hate? A troubled marriage? Your umpteenth year of singlehood? Believe that God has a plan and that He is going to use this season of your life as the catalyst for revealing it to you. Ask Him to give you a "God-awareness" so you can see His handiwork in every difficulty you encounter.

Rather than wishing you were married instead of single, in full-time ministry instead of corporate America, attending a big church instead of a small one, married to a saved spouse instead of an unsaved one, listen for what God is saying in your circumstances right now. Don't waste your time wishing; get busy looking and listening. Ask the Lord to open your ears to hear what He is saying to you right where you are.

> **HE SPEAKS:** *"We know that God causes everything to work together for the good of those who love God and are called according to his purpose for them."*
>
> —ROMANS 8:28

God Speaks to Us in the Present Tense

For years, Kimberly had looked for an opportunity to work in ministry. She sensed in Bible study and through the guidance of the Spirit that the Lord was leading her to minister to women, and she wanted to speak to women across the country in conference settings. She prayerfully offered these desires to the Lord for several years and even created a brochure on her ministry and sent it out to local churches, but she received very few responses.

Meanwhile, Kimberly's sixteen-year-old daughter had lots of friends who would visit their home. During their get-togethers, they would often engage Kimberly in conversation about spiritual matters. While Kimberly was spending time with the Lord one morning, it occurred to her that this group of young women was the one that God wanted her to minister to. He had given her a passion for women's ministry, and the women she was to minister to were already sitting right in her front room!

A SAINT SPEAKS: *"One of the best pieces of advice I ever got was 'Do the next thing.'"*

—ELISABETH ELLIOT

God is the God of *right now.* He doesn't want us to regret yesterday or worry about tomorrow. He wants us to focus on what He is saying to us and putting in front of us right now. The Enemy's voice will focus on the past and the future, but the voice of our God will focus on today. God's voice tells us what we can do now. Satan's voice tells us what we could do "if only."

Are you waiting for things to change before you try to discern God's voice? If so, maybe that's why things aren't changing. He's waiting for you to listen for Him now. His directions for the next season will come as you faithfully serve in the situation you're in right now.

Does Bible study seem dry? Does His voice seem far away? Keep studying. Keep listening. When God appears in something, just worship Him and expect that this is part of His plan for you. He has allowed you to be aware of His activity in order to point you to His plan for your life. Ask yourself:

- What persistent naggings have I recently been experiencing in my spirit?

- What events have reinforced what I'm sensing the Lord is asking me to do?

- What do I see God doing in my life?

- What do I hear God saying to me in my current circumstances?

- What do I plan to do right now as a result of what I'm hearing?

Walking in God's will for your life means following the leading of the Spirit minute by minute. Do you want to hear God's voice regarding His will for you? Then ask yourself what it is He has asked you to do *right now*. This is His will. Look to see where circumstances are leading you, and then ask yourself: "What do I need to do next?" Then do it. He will take it from there.

One of the clearest ways to discern God's voice is to take notice of the ways He externally repeats a message He has given you internally. The Holy Spirit works in our hearts, in the hearts of others, and in the events of our lives to point us toward God. He uses all these things to cause us to hear and heed His voice. God persistently calls you in an attempt to turn your ears and actions in His direction. Your personal circumstances are visible evidence that God is speaking to you and asking you to drop what you're doing and jump on board. Pay attention and choose now to obey.

HOW DO YOU KNOW IT'S GOD'S VOICE?

"When I hear the same thing from two or three different people in a very short period of time, I know the Lord is speaking to me. It's as clear as a Fed-Ex letter."

—STEVE FARRAR

PART THREE

Revealing God's Character

"I have loved you with an everlasting love; I have

drawn you with loving-kindness."

—JEREMIAH 31:3 (NIV)

"*I have loved you with an everlasting love . . . I have drawn you [to me]*"
Listen to that. Nothing can separate us from the love of God . . . this
is His promise to us. And because He loves us, one of God's greatest
desires is to make Himself known to us. He wants to lead us into a
more intimate relationship with Him. How amazing to think that the
God who created heaven and earth longs to have a friendship with us.

Scripture does not implicitly teach us how to discern God's voice.
Yet, it does direct us to develop and practice the disciplines that press
us into God's presence and a more personal relationship with Him. It
tells us to seek Him, pray without ceasing, meditate on Scripture, and
listen. The Word implies that a direct outpouring of intimacy with the
Almighty brings clarity to hearing His voice. A natural result of
knowing God will automatically be better communication with God.

As you press into God, you will become more acquainted with
His character. The more you know and believe to be true about who
God is and what He is able to do, the more willing you will be to be
obedient to what He is asking of you. We come to know God through
seeing His character revealed through our experiences with Him,
through His Word and His Spirit.

In the Old Testament, there was a barrier between God and His
followers. Only the priest had access to Him beyond the veil in the
temple. But God made a new covenant through Christ's death on the
cross. Now there is no barrier between God and those who believe.
Through the Holy Spirit living within us, we can have unparalleled
fellowship with His majesty.

A Saint Speaks

"*I know the Lord is speaking to me when there is a consistent,
clear impression in my heart often confirmed by a promise or
statement from the Word of God and accompanied by a sense
of 'rightness' and peace when I have obeyed. Through the
years I have learned that I am most sensitive to His voice
when I am pursuing intimate communion with Him.*"

—CRAWFORD LORITTS

7

A Revealing Voice

"I will give them a heart to know me,
that I am the LORD.*"*

—JEREMIAH 24:7 (NIV)

In July 2006, Jerry and I were considering acquiring some property for our ministry. We were concerned about the purchase and asked God for clear direction. Two days before we were to sign the contract, a woman we had never met before came to speak to us. She offered us a more expensive piece of property, but at a more reasonable rate than the one we were thinking about purchasing. Even though she would lose thousands of dollars on her property, she said God clearly revealed to her it was to be used for "Going Beyond Ministries."

While we rejoiced about the offer on the land, our real excitement was found in what this experience demonstrated about the character of God. He used this incident to speak to us about His faithfulness. We received more than just clarity and direction regarding our land purchase; we received divine insight into God Himself.

When God speaks, His voice will be revealing for He

passionately desires for us to know who He is. In fact, that's what salvation is all about—knowing God. Jesus said, "This is the way to have eternal life—to know you, the only true God, and Jesus Christ, the one you sent to earth" (John 17:3). God doesn't want you just to *hear* about Him or from Him; He wants you to *experience* Him in your life, so you will *know* Him.

When God instructs you to do something and you obey based on what you already know about Him, He moves your relationship with Him from a mental one to an *experiential* one that reveals even more about Him. As you move from knowing about God, to experiencing God, to knowing God, the more clearly you will discern His voice.

> **A SAINT SPEAKS:** *"A little knowledge of God is worth more than a great deal of knowledge about Him."*
>
> —J. I. PACKER

God's Attributes

In Scripture, people's names identify them and stand for something specific about their character. The same is true of God. The Bible uses many names for the Lord to help us know Him. Different circumstances elicit different names of God, not only in the lives of biblical characters but in our own lives as well. When Jerry and I followed God's leading in our circumstances, we experienced Him as *Jehovah-Jireh*—God Our Provider. Other believers in different situations experience other attributes of God.

When Hurricane Katrina struck, it completely destroyed Nancy and Jeff's home in Louisiana. But unlike many people, they didn't lose family members in the storm, and they felt blessed. Though they had limited resources, they sensed God leading them to help take care of families who had lost loved ones. It didn't seem rational to extend themselves to others when they were in need themselves, but this idea continued to permeate their thoughts.

As they sought God in prayer and Bible study, God spoke to them about His love for them, and that gave them the assurance they needed to do what He was asking of them. They decided that obeying God's voice, no matter how crazy it might appear to others, would enable them to experience God in a real and personal way. They believed that He would go before them and that His goodness and loving-kindness would follow them. So they moved forward in obedience to help the thousands of people displaced by the storm.

Since that time, Nancy and Jeff have experienced God's loving guidance and provision in ways they could never have imagined—from the free housing they received to the job opportunities that have replenished their finances. Now they not only know about God, but they have experienced Him in their lives. By seeking to experience God in their circumstances, they came to know Him as *Jehovah-Rohi*—Jehovah Our Shepherd.

> **HE SPEAKS**: *"The Lord is my shepherd, I shall not want. . . . Surely goodness and lovingkindness will follow me all the days of my life, and I will dwell in the house of the Lord forever."*
>
> —PSALM 23:1, 6 (NASB)

God reveals Himself in ways that are relevant to our circumstances. This means that those in the most challenging situations can expect to learn the most about God. You'd have to look a long time to find someone in worse circumstances than Job. In a very short period, this righteous man lost everything: his family, his money, and even his health. In the midst of all his suffering, Job tried to speak with God.

Well, actually, he tried to argue with God. He *demanded* to know why all this was happening to him. For a while God didn't say anything. He just sat back and listened to some of Job's friends tell him what *they* knew about God—most of which they got wrong. God finally spoke up. Against the backdrop of the circumstances of Job's life, God painted a portrait of Himself, so Job could see Him as He is. Through a series of questions, He revealed all the things about Himself that Job needed to know—His power, righteousness, omniscience, and sovereignty (Job 38–41).

Job got the message. When God had finished speaking, he said: "I had heard about you before, but now I have seen you with my own eyes. I take back everything I said, and I sit in dust and ashes to show my repentance" (Job 42:5–6).

Job had known *about God*, but his circumstances, crushing though they were, led him to *know God*. The Lord is *El-Shaddai*—the All-Sufficient God. Could this have been God's goal all along in allowing Job to suffer? Was it to get him to move from a mental knowing to an experiential one? I think so. God reveals His attributes to us because He wants us to know Him. Without knowledge of the nature of God, obedience to Him becomes more difficult, if not impossible. The more you know and believe to be true about who God is and what He can do, the more willing you become to obey what He commands.

God's Goal

When I picked up the phone to call Dr. Blackaby, I was on a mission to discover the secret behind the godly life of this incredible man of God and to glean his insights on discerning the voice of God.

"Mr. Blackaby," I began, "how do you know for sure when the Lord is speaking to you?" As if we were old friends, he shared many wonderful truths that I scribbled down as quickly as I could. He ended our phone call with these words: "Really, Priscilla, it's very simple! The more you know God, the better you will be able to discern His voice."

As I pondered those words over the next several days, I began to discern how important knowing Him is to recognizing Him when He speaks.

My brother, Anthony Evans Jr., is the spitting image of my father. Not only does he bear my father's name, but they also sound just alike. My brother has often used this to have fun at others' expense. Many times people will talk with Anthony on the phone for quite a while before they realize that they aren't speaking with my father. I have watched my brother trick even very close acquaintances by pretending to be my dad.

The apostle Paul warns us that Satan disguises himself as an angel of light (2 Corinthians 11:14). He deliberately tries to speak to us in a way that sounds like the Holy Spirit. But as hard as he tries to imitate the voice of God, he will never sound exactly like the real thing; and the more intimate we are with God, the more quickly we'll be able to tell who is really speaking. To recognize Satan's lies, all we have to do is spend our time in intimate fellowship with the Truth. When God speaks, His voice will reveal the same attributes as He reveals in His Word.

No matter how alike my brother's and father's voices sound, my brother can't fool me! Just a couple of seconds on the phone with him reveals to me exactly who is on the other end of the line. I have spent enough time with both of them to know the small but distinct differences in their voices.

God wants our relationship with Him to be so close that Satan's voice can never deceive us. If we focus on the priority of knowing Him, an automatic result will be that we more clearly hear God, discern His voice, and receive divine guidance for our lives.

God's Priorities

If we wish to discern God's voice, we must make His priorities our priorities. The first thing Paul asked when he met the risen Savior on the road to Damascus was, "Who are You, Lord?" (Acts 9:5 NASB). Later he wrote, "Nothing is as wonderful as knowing Christ Jesus my Lord. I have given up everything else and count it all as garbage. All I want is Christ" (Philippians 3:8 CEV).

Nothing, Paul says, is as wonderful as knowing God—not even hearing His voice and knowing His will. As precious as those things are, they were never Paul's primary goal because he understood that if he knew God, they would automatically follow. From the very beginning of his relationship with Christ, Paul had his priorities straight.

Pause a moment to take a personal inventory. Could it be that you can't discern God's voice because you have somehow bypassed the need to know who He really is? My conversation with Mr. Blackaby caused me to question my own priorities. Was I voice hunting more than I was God hunting? Had knowing His will taken precedent over just knowing

Him? With the tender conviction that comes only from God Himself, I quickly discovered that my focus had been on the wrong thing.

> **A SAINT SPEAKS:** *"Whoever seeks God as a means toward desired ends will not find God. The mighty God, the maker of heaven and earth, will not be one of many treasures, not even the chief of all treasures. He will be all in all or He will be nothing."*
>
> —A. W. TOZER

Often what we want to know most is where God wants us to go and what He wants us to do—or even what He wants to do for us! We tend to seek God's direction or blessings more than we seek Him. But God wants us to know how to discern His voice as a result of knowing *Him.* When you make knowing God your priority, He will reveal truths about Himself that will point to the path you should take, and when you take it, His blessings will follow.

King David's life illustrates this principle clearly. "With all my heart I have sought You," he wrote (Psalm 119:10 NASB). These passionate words came from the lips of a man who had just described all the distressing circumstances of his life. His own family despised him, and the king of Israel was trying to kill him. He had fallen into a deep pit of sin and experienced the silence of God. The wicked were prospering while God's people were floundering. Despite all this, David's number-one priority was to know God.

David's focus wasn't on his circumstances or what he expected God to do about them; it was on God Himself. He never became so disillusioned with the circumstances of his life that he stopped seeking to know God. Even when he felt as if God was no longer speaking and he couldn't figure out why, the consuming passion of his heart was still to follow hard after God.

You know when you're seeking something other than God when you're in one of those "in-between" stages where nothing seems to be happening and God doesn't seem to be speaking, so you stop pursuing Him. This indicates that you're more interested in what you think He is going to do for you than you are in knowing Him in order to have an intimate relationship with Him. To discern God's voice, you have to get your priorities straight. You have to want Him, His glory, and a relationship with Him more than you want anything else.

> **A SAINT SPEAKS:** *"There is no sweeter manner of living in the world than continuous communion with God. Only those who have experienced it can understand. However, I don't advise you to practice it for the sole purpose of gaining consolation from your problems. Seek it, rather because God wills it and out of love for Him."*
>
> —BROTHER LAWRENCE

God's Responsibilities

David concluded Psalm 119:10 (NASB) with these words: "Do not let me wander from Your commandments." Notice that he puts the responsibility for staying in the will of God on God Himself. He says, "You, God— please don't let me wander from Your will!" Our responsibility is to get to know God. His is to keep us from wandering from His will for our lives.

When I'm crossing a street with my little boys, I hold each firmly by the hand to make sure they get safely to our destination. Because they are children, it isn't their responsibility to stay with me as much as it is my responsibility, as their mother, to keep them from wandering.

This task is normally easier for me with Jackson than with Jerry Jr. Jackson won't let go of my hand to go in another direction without first getting my nod of approval. Jerry Jr. is another story. He doesn't care whether he has my approval or not. When he wants to head in a different direction, he just scampers away as fast as his little legs can carry him.

Some of us are like Jackson in our relationship with God. We aren't perfect, but it is our natural inclination to check with God before scampering away. But others of us, like Jerry Jr., run quickly from His side the minute something captures our attention. In either case, God knows our temperament, and as long as our priority is to know Him, He takes it upon Himself to hold us in a firm grip to make sure that we don't wander from His will.

Are you desperately seeking to know the will of God for your life? Are you in bondage because you can't take a step in any direction without being afraid that you'll wander from His will? If so, here is the truth that will set you free: *It is God's responsibility to cause you to hear and recognize His voice.* He wants to reveal His will to you, and Scripture clearly shows that He will do it:

- Proverbs 3:6 (NKJV)—"In all your ways acknowledge Him, and He shall direct your paths."

- Philippians 3:15 (NASB)—"Let us therefore, as many as are perfect [mature] have this attitude and if in anything you have a different attitude, God will reveal that also to you."

- Philippians 2:13 (NIV)— "It is God who works in you to will and to act according to his good purpose."

Listen to the words of the psalmist in Psalm 37:14 (NASB), "Delight yourself in the Lord, and He will give you the desires of your heart." Once again, we find God's promise to steer our desires in the direction of His will if we will just get down to the business of delighting in Him.

Many of us suspect that God is doing everything in His power to keep us from discovering His will. On the contrary, He is doing everything in His power to reveal it and cause us to go after it!

If you keep seeking God, He will continue to develop your awareness of who He is and His will for you. As you study His Word, listen to His revealing voice. Ask yourself, "What does this teach me about the character of God?" Make knowing Him your goal. Seek a Person instead of a plan. Seek a relationship instead of a road map. The closer you get to God, the more He will reveal Himself to you, and the natural result of knowing Him better will be a greater ability to discern His voice.

HOW DO YOU KNOW IT'S GOD'S VOICE?

"I know God is speaking when what I hear is consistent with what I know about Him. I remember a time when someone told me something my husband Keith said. It wasn't negative. It just didn't sound like him. I found out later it was a different Keith Moore. I knew deep inside that wasn't my man. Likewise we can know deep inside, 'That just isn't my God.' I've got to know God and His Word well enough to know what 'sounds' like Him and what doesn't. He never speaks contrary to His Word and His character."

—BETH MOORE

8

A Peaceful Voice

"I have told you all this so that you may have peace in me."

—JOHN 16:33

When my father was a young preacher in Dallas, the Lord gave him a vision for ministry. Tony Evans believed that God wanted his small church to own not only the building in which they met for services but also the street on which it was located, so the church could minister to the community through the businesses there. Many people in the congregation didn't believe this was possible because there was no money to buy the land.

Despite the naysayers, my father moved forward in faith and obedience, expecting to see God's supernatural activity. God moved, and today Oak Cliff Bible Fellowship owns the street on which it sits, as well as many of the businesses on that street. My father persisted because God's peace ruled in his heart. That peace assured him that he had heard from God and that this is what He wanted him to do.

A SAINT SPEAKS: *"Peace and truth are the great subject matter of divine revelation . . . truth to direct us, peace to make us easy."*

—MATTHEW HENRY

Before Jesus died, He comforted His disciples by telling them that His peace would remain with them even after He was gone. He wanted us to have real peace—a permanent restful assurance that nothing can diminish or destroy because it rests deep in our souls. "I am leaving you with a gift—peace of mind and heart," He said. "And the peace I give isn't like the peace the world gives. So don't be troubled or afraid" (John 14:27). The Lord was assuring His disciples that with *real* peace not even dreadful circumstances could destroy their serenity.

The Lord was so focused on peace that His first words to the disciples after the resurrection were "Peace be with you" (John 20:19). And again after showing them His pierced hands and feet, He said, "Peace be with you" (v. 21). Moments later, He breathed on them and gave them the gift of peace in the person of the Holy Spirit (v. 22). When God speaks to you, you'll recognize His voice because the Holy Spirit will release a peaceful assurance as He leads you to make God-honoring decisions.

Peace is a gift that accompanies your salvation. It is one of the great blessings from our Father to His children. *Jehovah Shalom*—the God of Peace—is one of the names that depict God's character. When you accepted Christ as your Savior, you received the Holy Spirit (Romans 8:9) and the Holy Spirit embodies peace.

Ruling Peace

As my husband and I courted and moved toward marriage, I was terrified. I thought that Jerry was a wonderful man and would make an incredible husband, but I had no confidence in my own ability to meet all of the demands of married life. In fact the idea of being a wife terrified me!

After praying and seeking wise counsel, I really began to feel that the Holy Spirit was guiding me to marry Jerry. Despite my lack of self-confidence, as I continued praying, the Holy Sprit gave me a sense of peace to confirm that I had indeed heard His direction correctly. This enabled me to move forward, trusting in God's ability to carry me through, regardless of how inadequate I felt for the task ahead. Such peace comes only from God.

As you learn to discern God's voice through His character, one of the ways you will know He is speaking is when you sense His peace about the things that He is asking you to do. Even when you step out to do something that seems impossible, if it's God's will for you, His peace will accompany your actions. You may not feel confident in your own ability, but you will feel confident about His.

When the Holy Spirit takes up residence in you and awakens your conscience from its spiritual slumber, He begins to use it to lead you into God's will.

When Colossians 3:15 says, "Let the peace that comes from Christ rule in your hearts," it means that peace is not to just *be a part* of our lives; it is *to rule* in our lives. We need to pay close attention to see if peace reigns in our soul when we make decisions or act in a certain way. We can't lose the God-given peace we have as Christians, but if we're contemplating doing something that isn't pleasing to God, peace won't rule.

In baseball, the umpire behind home plate is the one who decides when a pitch is in or out of the strike zone. As the Umpire of our hearts, the Holy Spirit is the One who decides whether we are in or out of God's will. When we're being obedient to God's will, the Holy Spirit reassures us by giving us a sense of inner tranquility. When we step outside of His will, even by accident, we lose that feeling of serenity.

When you feel a contest going on in your heart, you need to pay close attention. God is speaking. The Holy Spirit is trying to make the call for you and lead you to make a correct decision. There's nothing to compare with experiencing the peace that comes from choosing to yield to the Umpire of your heart.

A SAINT SPEAKS: *"A reigning sense of God's peace confirms His voice to me. There may have been internal turmoil getting to that peace, but when I have settled in on His desire for me, I am assured of that by the peace that accompanies it."*

—KAY ARTHUR

Relational Peace

In college I belonged to a wonderful Christian sorority. The goal of this association was to provide an alternative for Christian women who didn't want to be involved in secular sororities. I enjoyed my time with this group, but I also wanted to join another sorority on campus. There were many girls in the Christian sorority who genuinely believed that joining the other group would be displeasing to God. On the other hand, I believed that this was a matter of personal conviction and that the Lord had given me the freedom to join, and I did.

The ripple effect my decision had on the girls in my Christian sorority was amazing. Feelings were hurt, questions were raised, and concerns expressed. The worst part was that many of them were fledgling believers who struggled to make sense of what I had done. As I look back after all these years, I see that although God had given me freedom in that area, exercising my freedom caused other Christians to stumble.

HE SPEAKS: *"The wisdom that comes from heaven is first of all pure. It is also peace loving, gentle at all times, and willing to yield to others."*

—JAMES 3:17

One of the contentious issues in the early church was whether or not it was all right for Christians to eat food that had been offered to idols. The apostle Paul taught that individual Christians had the liberty to follow their own conscience in the matter, but he also pointed to the deeper issue: "Let us aim for harmony in the church and try to build each other up. Don't tear apart the work of God over what you eat. Remember, there is nothing wrong with these things in themselves. But it is wrong to eat anything if it makes another person stumble. Don't eat meat, or drink wine, or do anything else if it might cause another Christian to stumble" (Romans 14:19–21).

Paul says that pursuing peace and building each other up are much more important than a trivial issue like what to eat. Notice the key words "or do anything else." Before we exercise our freedoms, we need to consider how they will affect those around us. God will never want us to behave in a way that can harm other believers. When the Holy Spirit opens our eyes to see that a fellow believer will be hurt by what we are about to do, He is telling us, "Not now!" This doesn't mean that we have lost that freedom. We just aren't supposed to enjoy it right then. Preserving a fellow believer from stumbling trumps our personal freedoms.

As you seek to be careful about enjoying your freedoms, be sure not to impede the spiritual progress of Christians who are growing spiritually. Such people have done more than just accept Christ as Savior. They have clearly demonstrated that they're on a journey with God and are moving forward in their relationship with Him. That's the kind of people the women in my Christian sorority were. They loved the Lord and were truly seeking His will in the matter. I now believe I was a stumbling block to them because my decision shook their faith and confidence in their relationship with God.

Peaceable relationships are important to God. Therefore, we can conclude that the Holy Spirit will not lead us to do anything that in any way hinders peace and unity in the body of Christ. This doesn't mean that everyone will always agree with what you're doing, but it does mean that your decision won't cause another believer to stumble.

HE SPEAKS: *"Always keep yourselves united in the Holy Spirit, and bind yourselves together with peace."*

—EPHESIANS 4:3

A word of caution: If you're not careful, the Enemy can make the pressure of keeping your fellow believers safe an area of bondage for you. Before you know it, you'll no longer be able to enjoy any freedoms because you'll be constantly worrying about how it will affect others.

Paul's use of the mental image of a "stumbling block" shows us how to prevent this. The picture he paints is one of people who are moving forward but who lose their balance and fall because someone has done something that caused them to stumble. This means that God wants us to encourage and support those who are growing in their faith, not hinder them. As you seek to determine God's leading, ask yourself, "Although there are some who may not agree with my freedom, is there anyone whose spiritual growth will be hindered by my choice?" If there is, then wisely choose to forgo your freedom to encourage their spiritual growth.

> **A SAINT SPEAKS:** *"You can always tell when a church or a family follows false wisdom: you will find jealousy, division, and confusion."*
>
> —WARREN WIERSBY

Ruptured Peace

Warfare is a fact of life, and Scripture makes it clear that it isn't just between nations or unbelievers. Believers also quarrel, fight, and kill:

- Cain slew Abel. (Genesis 4:8)

- Absalom rebelled against his father, David. (2 Samuel 15:10)

- Jesus' disciples argued about who would be greatest. (Luke 9:46)

- Believers at Corinth sued one another. (1 Corinthians 6:6)

- Eudoia and Syntyche weren't on speaking terms. (Philippians 4:2)

If God has called us to peace and given us the gift of peace at salvation, how can such things be? James says that all external wars are the result of a war being waged within the individual soul. "What causes fights and quarrels among you?" he asks. "Don't they come from your desires that battle within you?" (James 4:1 NIV). As the cartoon character Pogo put it, "We have met the enemy, and he is us."

A civil war is raging within as the still unsanctified parts of our soul fight to fulfill the lusts of the flesh. Unbelievers can't help themselves. As long as they are still at war with God, they will always be at war with themselves and with others. The sin nature naturally covets and quarrels and kills to get what it wants. Believers, on the other hand, have a Helper— God Himself.

> **HE SPEAKS:** *"Oh, that you had listened to my commands!*
> *Then you would have had peace flowing like a gentle river*
> *and righteousness rolling like waves."*
>
> —ISAIAH 48:18

The Holy Spirit contends mightily against our selfish desires, for they are in direct conflict with what He wants us to be and do. Discord and righteousness are irreconcilable; they cannot coexist. But if we are to have peace, we must cooperate with the Spirit, and this can be hard work. Paul tells us that we must *"make every effort to do what leads to peace"* (Romans 14:19 NIV). James gets more specific. In James 4:7 through 10 (NIV), he tells us to:

- Submit ourselves to God. (Obey Him.)

- Resist the devil. (Don't buy into Satan's lies.)

- Come near to God. (Reverence God for who He is.)

- Wash our hands. (Allow the blood of Christ to cleanse our conscience.)

- Purify our hearts. (Let the truth of His Word sanctify our intentions.)

- Grieve, mourn, and wail. (Sincerely repent of our sins.)

- Humble ourselves. (Admit our dependence on God.)

These instructions should sound very familiar by now. They are the very things that prepare us to hear from God and enable us to discern His voice when He speaks. If you're willing to obey them, the Holy Spirit will give you the power to follow them. When you do, the Devil will flee and God will draw near to you. He will cleanse you, forgive you, and restore your peace.

God's voice is peaceful. It will always lead you in the direction of internal and external peace, and a sense of peace and assurance will always accompany His personal word to you.

HOW DO YOU KNOW IT'S GOD'S VOICE?

"I know the Lord is speaking when I have a complete sense of peace, a sense of rightness at the very center of my being. Although I don't hear an audible voice, I feel a definite 'yes!' in my spirit. Not only will His unspoken words ring true, spiritually and emotionally, but they will also stand in total agreement with His written words in the Bible. For confirmation that it's the Lord's voice and not my own fleshly desires leading me, I pray, search the Scriptures, then share what I believe God has revealed to me with someone I trust. If their immediate response is, 'Yes, absolutely!' then I can move forward with confidence."

—LIZ CURTIS HIGGS

9

A Truthful Voice

*"God's voice thunders in marvelous
ways; he does great things beyond
our understanding."*

—JOB 37:5 (NIV)

When I was little and my mother had to leave me some-
where for a short time, she would always squat down in front
of me, look me square in the eye, and say, "Priscilla, you stay
here until I get back. Don't go with anybody. Don't let anyone
tell you that I sent them to get you. I'm not sending anybody.
You stay here and wait for me."

I had my mother's word on that. She had made it clear.
There was no need to question it. If anyone said anything to
me that was contrary to what she had said, I would know they
weren't telling the truth because she had already spoken on that
issue, and she would stand behind her word.

God stands behind His Word. When we read Scriptures,
it's as if He is squatting down in front of us, putting our face
in His hands, and saying, "This is who I am, and this is what
I am going to do. Don't let anybody tell you differently. Believe Me." Anyone who refuses to act on the knowledge God

reveals in Scripture will never know how to discern His voice. Where the Scriptures are ignored, He remains the unknown God.

One of the distinguishing characteristics of God's voice is that it is completely truthful. It will never contradict His written Word or His character. God is "the God of truth" (Psalm 31:5 NIV), so when you hear the voice of God through the Holy Spirit and the Word, you can be certain it will always lead you in the direction of truth. In a world that has determined there are no absolutes by which we can measure truth, the believer resolutely places his sole standard of genuine accuracy on the Bible. This kind of truth doesn't depend on how you feel or what you think, because whether you believe it or not, it is pure truth.

> **HE SPEAKS:** *"Let those who are wise understand these things. Let those who are discerning listen carefully."*
>
> —Hosea 14:9

God's Pure Truth

As Tara and I talked about her decision to move in with her fiancé, my patience grew thin. By taking Scripture references out of context and applying them inappropriately, she had woven a web of rationalizations to excuse her actions. Now with great self-assurance, she tried to elicit an approving response from me.

She was certain that she had heard from God and that He was not only allowing but also blessing her union with this young man. As I listened, I thought about when Tara had accepted Christ and the spiritual fruit her salvation had produced. Knowing that the Holy Spirit lived in her, I wondered how she could be so off base when it came to discerning God's voice.

Tara might have felt led to do what she had chosen to do, but I can guarantee that the Holy Spirit wasn't the One leading her. She could not have heard the Spirit of truth because He speaks only what He hears from God. And God never speaks contrary to His written Word. Yet what Tara heard obviously contradicted what God has revealed in Scripture.

We have all been in this position at one time or another. Our circumstances may have been different, but our problem was the same. We thought for certain God was saying something that He wasn't. How can we clearly discern His voice from our own desires? The simplest way is to see what His Word says is true.

While He was on earth, Jesus said over and over again, "I am telling you the truth." As He prepared to return to the Father, He told His disciples: "When the Spirit of truth comes, he will guide you into all truth" (John 16:13).

The Greek word for *truth* in this verse denotes a two-plus-two-equals-four kind of truth. It means a truth that has no mixture of bias, pretense, falsehood, or deceit. When you hear the voice of the Holy Spirit, you can be certain that what He says is the truth, the whole truth, and nothing but the truth.

The Holy Spirit who lives inside of you never speaks to you without having received direct revelation from God. He doesn't create messages on His own initiative. Every message He delivers to you comes straight from the God of truth. This is great news for those of us who desire to know the will of God for us. The Holy Spirit is the only One who has direct access to the truth of God's thoughts concerning you, and He has a desire to share these revelations.

> **HE SPEAKS:** *"The Spirit searches all things, even the depths of God. . . . Now we have received, not the spirit of the world, but the Spirit who is from God, so that we may know the things freely given to us by God."*
>
> —1 CORINTHIANS 2:10–12 (NASB)

Satan, the great deceiver, wants you to think God's written Word is *not* absolutely true. Friend, if you allow the Enemy to get away with this, you'll never be able to clearly discern God's voice. Satan wants you to create your own standard of truth by picking and choosing what you want to hear. One of the primary ways he does this is by tempting you to substitute human traditions for God's truth. This is what Tara was doing.

My conversation with her revealed that most of the women in her family had lived with their husbands before they married them. She had learned this behavior and had become comfortable with it. My goal was to help her realize that no matter how deeply woven into the fabric of her life her family traditions were, they didn't override God's truth. This can be a hard concept to swallow for those who have been raised with strong family or cultural traditions. It certainly was hard for the apostle Peter.

According to traditional Jewish culture, it wasn't okay to eat certain foods. But when Christ came, He gave His followers permission to eat foods that had previously been considered unclean. Paul told Timothy that "God created those foods to be eaten with thanksgiving by people who know and believe the truth" (1 Timothy 4:3).

Believers who had a Gentile upbringing relished their liberty in Christ to freely eat all things. But Jewish believers, who had been raised to observe dietary restrictions, still often felt convicted about eating certain foods. One day, while dining with some Gentiles, Peter ate some of these foods. All was well until some of his friends from his old neighborhood showed up and saw what he was doing. Suddenly Peter allowed the traditions of his culture to override the truth, and he distanced himself from the Gentiles he had just shared a meal with. Paul called Peter on the carpet for his hypocrisy. He told him that he wasn't being "straightforward about the truth of the gospel" (Galatians 2:14 NASB).

> **A SAINT SPEAKS:** *"The Bible is God's message to everybody. We deceive ourselves if we claim to want to hear His voice but neglect the primary channel through which it comes. We must read His Word. We must obey it. We must live it, which means rereading it throughout our lives."*
>
> —ELISABETH ELLIOT

Since traditions shape our thinking, it can be easy for us to lean on our own understanding and assume that it is okay for us to do what we've been taught to do or what we're used to doing. But God's standard of truth is often very different from the one our family, culture, or perhaps even our denomination teaches. Just because we feel comfortable doing something doesn't make it right. We must filter it through God's revealed truth: His Word. *Anything* you hear that contradicts Scripture is not from Him.

If you are currently struggling with a decision and are confused as to whether the voice you are hearing is coming from the Spirit of Truth, ask yourself these questions:

- Will it contradict the truth found in Scripture?

- Will it cause me to indulge in sin of any kind?

- Will it encourage me to hypocritically cover up my sin?

- Will it give glory to God by magnifying His truth to the people involved?

Filtered through the truth of God's Word and His Spirit, you should be able to determine if you are acting according to God's will.

> **A SAINT SPEAKS:** *"To His Word we may always go with prayerful expectation. . . . We are to study and know the Scriptures that every word of His testimony may instruct us."*
>
> —LEWIS SPERRY CHAFER

Strongholds against Truth

One night while watching a documentary on TV, I was riveted by the story of a beautiful young woman who was molested as a child. As a result of that abuse, thoughts of guilt and shame exalted themselves in her mind. These strongholds got so big that the only relief she found was in mutilating herself. Strongholds were literally destroying her.

Strongholds are barricades that keep the voice of God from reaching our spiritual ears. They are constructed from rebellious thoughts that are contrary to the Word of God. In 2 Corinthians 10:4–5 (NASB), Paul calls these rebellious ideas, "fortresses," "speculations," and "lofty things." He clearly states that these strongholds have a specific purpose: to stand up "against the knowledge of God."

Paul wants to reveal that strongholds set themselves up as towering structures in our souls for the purpose of standing against the knowledge of the freely given truth of God. Because they are the Devil's strongholds, they are lies, just as Satan was a liar from the beginning. If we wish to clearly discern God's voice, we *must* demolish them.

Thankfully, God has clearly shown us the weapons we need to do this. These weapons aren't your personal credentials or self-help resources. Relying on this sort of thing is like pulling weeds out of the ground without destroying the roots. The weeds just keep coming back because the remedy doesn't get to the source of the problem.

When you're dealing with the flesh, you can fight with the weapons of the flesh, but when you are fighting in the spiritual realm, you have to use divine weapons. Ephesians 6:10–20 outlines in detail the spiritual armor that we are to gird ourselves with in order to be prepared for battle. Everything listed in that passage is defensive in nature except one. The only offensive item listed is the sword of the Spirit: "Take the sword of the Spirit, which is the word of God" (v. 17). To demolish Satan's lies, you must rely on the truths of God's Word.

- When your stronghold says, "God could never love you," you say, "He loves me with an everlasting love" (Jeremiah 31:3).

- When your stronghold says, "God will never accept you," you say, "I am accepted because of my relationship with Christ" (Galatians 2:16).

- When your stronghold says, "You'll never be able to do that," you say, "I can do everything with the help of Christ who gives me the strength I need" (Philippians 4:13).

- When your stronghold says, "You're ugly," you say, "He delights in my beauty" (Psalm 45:11).

If we take time to carefully consider some of the ills we face, we may be able to trace them back to a stronghold that the Enemy has constructed to stand as a barrier against God's voice. A detrimental relationship might begin with the foundational belief that: "I don't deserve any better." A substance addiction might be traceable to a belief that: "I can only find peace in a bottle." A weight problem may start when a woman convinces herself that: "I have no self-control." The Enemy's goal is to keep our lives so full of these strongholds that we not only experience outward defeat but hamper our internal ability to hear God.

You demolish strongholds by consciously and consistently taking your thoughts captive with the truths of God's Word. You overthrow the authority of strongholds by replacing Satan's lies with the truths of Scripture.

HE SPEAKS: *"The word of the Lord holds true, and everything he does is worthy of our trust."*

—PSALM 33:4

A young lady named Libby e-mailed me recently to tell me about the problems that strongholds had created in her life and how she set about freeing herself from them.

Libby had a difficult childhood caused by her parents' terrible marriage and eventual divorce. During the marriage, her father committed adultery many times. Both during the marriage and after the divorce, her parents used Libby and her brother to manipulate and hurt each other. She grew up feeling abandoned, wronged, unprotected, and unloved. Tortured by feelings of low self-esteem and self-doubt, Libby developed many problems including an eating disorder, difficulty with relationships, and depression.

Libby's life began to change, though, when she had an encounter with God. After asking Him into her life, she found a sense of peace she'd never known before. As she grew in her relationship with Him, she desired to more clearly hear God's voice.

Libby realized that her strongholds were hampering her spiritual growth. With the Spirit's prompting, she understood she needed God's

Word in her heart to ward off Satan's hold over her. She began a rigorous discipline of Scripture memorization. Every hour on the hour, she would repeat the same verse three times—often setting her alarm to remind her. At the end of the week, each verse was written on an index card and filed by subject matter for future battles.

For the first few weeks, Libby continued to struggle with her problems. But then hope began to replace depression and a holy strength began to fill her. "The lies were quieting and His truth was ringing loudly," Libby said. "The destructive voices in my head were replaced by His and the Prince of Peace claimed my heart. I have continued to live triumphantly in Him since then."

Libby no longer experiences the depression that once had such a hold on her life. Now when she feels a stronghold threatening her, she battles with the sword of truth. She testifies, "Scripture is incredibly powerful!"

Libby took seriously the war that was raging and invested time and energy in the destruction of the strongholds that plagued her.

God's Truth in Assuring

Like Libby, the more acquainted you become with God's Word, the more accurately you will be able to distinguish His voice from the Enemy's. In a world full of sin and pride, it can be difficult to know when God is speaking. However, since the Word of God is the chief means through which He speaks, we can be certain to hear God most clearly when we remain consistent in our study of and meditation on His Word.

When you are filled with self-doubt, unsure what to do, what to think, or who to believe, it is a great comfort to know that you can count on God's Word. When God speaks, He is bound to do everything He says. His promises are sure. Please know that when you choose to rely on His standards instead of your own and follow His leading in obedience, He won't let you down. You'll see the glorious results that come only when you rely on God's absolute truth.

HOW DO YOU KNOW IT'S GOD'S VOICE?

"I know the Lord is speaking to me when what I think He is saying is driven home by Scripture. Once, when I was in England, I wondered whether to go into some pubs to talk to the kids there. I worried about my reputation. What would people think if they saw me going into those places? As I sought to find what was the 'right,' not the 'comfortable,' thing to do, I read in Philippians 2: 'He made Himself of no reputation.' So the still voice said to my soul, 'What are you worrying about your reputation for?' I went."

—JILL BRISCO

10

A Powerful Voice

*"The voice of the Lord echoes above the sea.
The God of glory thunders. The Lord thun-
ders above the mighty sea. The voice of the
Lord is powerful."*

—PSALM 29:3–4

As the waves crashed against the side of the cruise ship, my family and I held on to the sides of our chairs to try to keep from being thrown across our small cabin. We were right in the middle of a violent storm, and our dream family vacation was turning into a nightmare. Forty-foot waves were tossing the ship around as if it were a small wooden canoe. Huddled near the window, all I could see was the raging sea. I watched in amazement as the once calm seas revealed their life-threatening muscle and power. The ocean roared its authority, and we knew we were at its mercy. For the first time, I understood the awesome power of waves and wind and the terrifying strength of the ocean.

That day, God used the force of the storm to demonstrate a powerful lesson about His voice. The Holy Spirit reminded me of the words of Psalm 29, "The voice of the Lord echoes above the sea. . . . The voice of the Lord is powerful."

When God speaks, His voice has even more power and authority than the mighty waves that tossed our cruise ship to and fro. God is the One who commands the sea itself. He is *Jehovah Elohim*—the All-Powerful God. This form of God's name is used more than 2,500 times in the Bible. It stands for His powerful authority to make things happen. God clearly wants us to understand that *everything* is at the mercy of His Word. When God speaks, things change.

> **HE SPEAKS:** *"Yours, O LORD, is the greatness and the power and the glory and the majesty and the splendor, for everything in heaven and earth is yours. Yours, O LORD, is the kingdom; you are exalted as head over all."*
>
> —1 CHRONICLES 29:11

My friend Peg experienced the power of God's voice during a crisis time in her life. While on an out-of-state business trip, her husband Bob had a terrible accident that resulted in severe hemorrhaging in his brain. She was told by the neurosurgeon that there was a very strong possibility that her husband might not survive. And if he did live, Bob would probably have loss of speech and the use of the right side of his body.

From the moment she learned of the accident, Peg began to pray. She was so frightened she could scarcely form the words. But as Peg called out to God, she recalled the words of Romans 8:26, "And the Holy Spirit helps us in our distress. For we don't even know what we should pray for, nor how we should pray. But the Holy Spirit prays for us with groanings that cannot be expressed in words." So she simply prayed for the Spirit to intervene for Bob.

While on the plane traveling to reach the hospital, Peg's heart was racing so fast that she feared a heart attack. Unless she regained control of her emotions, she knew she wouldn't be able to provide the help and assurance her husband was certain to need. She called out to God to strengthen and calm her. At that moment, she clearly heard a voice speak, "All is well!"

As my friend tells this story, she relates that what happened next was like someone flipping a switch inside her body. Her heartbeat immediately returned to normal, and she experienced the most extreme peace she had ever known. God spoke and instantly things changed. While Peg didn't know then if "all is well" meant her husband would be well or if God was assuring her of His presence and authority, she trusted God's word and believed that, whatever the outcome, all would be well.

Today Bob is completely healthy and totally recovered. He shows no indication of ever having had a brain injury. When a doctor later reviewed a follow-up brain scan, he shook his head in puzzlement. "It's miraculous," he told Bob and Peg. "I see the damage in the brain, but you don't show any of the effects that should be evident." They knew it was, indeed, a miracle. God spoke and His mighty power was evidenced.

Nothing can remain the same when His mighty voice is heard. A look at the Scriptures quickly reveals what God's powerful voice can do. Just a few examples show us His voice:

- Created the waters (Genesis 1:7)

- Divided the water from the dry land (Genesis 1:9)

- Created a human being out of dust (Genesis 2)

- Imposed order out of chaos (Genesis 1)

- Spoke peace to a storm (Mark 4)

- Brought a man back from death (John 11)

- Caused the Enemy to flee (Matthew 4)

- Called a woman out from her hiding place (Mark 5)

- Instantly forgave sin (John 8)

The Gospel accounts of Jesus' miracles teach us some important lessons about how we can discern God's voice and experience its power in a way that brings Him glory. Let's look closely at one of the most familiar stories in the Bible in which the power of God's voice is seen.

A SAINT SPEAKS: *"Things don't change when I talk to God; things change when God talks to me. When I talk, nothing happens; when God talks, the universe comes into existence."*

—BOB SORGE

Observing the Effect of God's Word

The gospel of Mark says that one night when Jesus and His disciples were crossing the Sea of Galilee, a violent storm suddenly arose. Jesus was asleep on a cushion in the stern, and in their panic, the disciples awakened Him. When Jesus woke up, He "rebuked the wind and said to the water, 'Quiet down!' Suddenly the wind stopped, and there was a great calm" (Mark 4:39).

One of the clearest ways we can separate God's voice from that of the Enemy's is by the effect it has on us and our circumstances. God's Word always produces clear results. As you seek to discern His voice, ask yourself: "Is the effect I'm seeing very noticeable?" When Jesus calmed the waves, the change was obvious. One of the evidences that God has spoken is when things in our lives change dramatically.

During the height of Dwight L. Moody's ministry, he led thousands of people to the Lord. Many, including Moody, were astounded at the unbelievable fruit that his messages were producing in the lives of those who heard it. When asked about this, Moody would always point to a sacred encounter he had with God. During it, God clearly spoke to his heart and he emerged forever changed. He always asserted that meeting with God was the turning point that began his revolutionary ministry, which produced such dramatic results.

I have witnessed this same revolutionary change myself. Recently a young woman whom I knew in high school walked up to say hello after a Sunday morning service. I hadn't seen Yvonne for more than a decade, so I didn't recognize her immediately. She hadn't changed much physically, but there was clearly something different about her. The memory I have of her from high school was of an angry, self-centered girl who always kept people at arm's length. She never had a warm expression or a kind word to say. She was tough and insensitive. But now a totally different woman stood before me. Her countenance had changed. The icy exterior was gone. She actually glowed!

Our quick conversation revealed the reason for the change: Yvonne had heard the powerful voice of God, and it had calmed the raging within. God's voice had done in Yvonne's life what Jesus' voice had done to the roaring waters of the Sea of Galilee, and it was obvious to everyone that He had changed her life.

Although sometimes we have to wait to see the impact of God's word, many times the effect of His voice is immediate. When Jesus spoke to the wind and the waves, they *immediately* became still. As you seek to discern His voice, ask yourself, "Is the effect I'm seeing happening quickly?"

When I see things changing rapidly with no help from me, I know the Lord has spoken and that He is up to something. When He begins to move, the results will be both immediate and obvious. You will know beyond a doubt that God is performing what He has spoken. And often the first change you'll see won't be in your circumstances. It will be in *you!*

> **A SAINT SPEAKS:** *"The Old Testament depicted God's utterance, the actual statement of His purpose, as having power in itself to effect the thing purposed. . . . The Word of God is thus God at work."*
>
> —J. I. PACKER

Michael had been married for five years when his marriage began to struggle. He felt his love for his wife waning. She was difficult to live with, and her nagging voice grated on his nerves. Michael took his concerns to the Lord and asked Him to speak to his circumstances.

One day, Michael spent several hours pursuing God and His solution to the problem. While he was searching Scripture, the Holy Spirit reminded him of the Lord's undying, all-encompassing love for him.

Michael remembered how God had given His life for him even though he didn't deserve it. As the Holy Spirit spoke, Michael heard from God. He knew God was asking him to love his wife the same way that God loved him—unconditionally and completely—and he asked the Lord to help him see his wife through His eyes.

When he emerged from his time with the Lord, Michael noticed a change. He immediately saw his wife in a brand-new way. She was the same and their marriage was the same, but he was different. God's voice had changed *him*. Now, thirty-five years later, both Michael and his wife are a testimony to the obvious and immediate results of God's powerful word.

Demonstrating the Purpose of God's Word

Remember that the Holy Spirit speaks in order to glorify the Father. That is His goal. We can recognize that God has spoken when there is an obvious change that leads us and others to focus our attention on Him, learn more about Him, and praise Him.

When Jesus spoke to heal the sick, everybody nearby could see the results, and the authors of the Gospel accounts give many instances of witnesses glorifying God for what He had done:

- Matthew says that when Jesus' word made a mute man talk by casting a demon out of him, "the crowds marveled. 'Nothing like this has ever happened in Israel!' they exclaimed" (Matthew 9:33).

- Mark says that when Jesus' word cast an evil spirit out of a man, "amazement gripped the audience, and they began to discuss what had happened. 'What sort of new teaching is this?' they asked excitedly. 'It has such authority!'" (Mark 1:27).

- Luke says that that when Jesus' word healed a paralytic, "everyone was gripped with great wonder and awe. And they praised

God, saying over and over again, 'We have seen amazing things today'" (Luke 5:26).

- John says that when Jesus' word healed the centurion's son, "the officer and his entire household believed in Jesus" (John 4:53).

While many gave God the glory for the powerful results of His word, others denied that Jesus was God. Some said with the Pharisees, "He can cast out demons because he is empowered by the prince of demons" (Matthew 9:34). In the face of this kind of unbelief, Jesus often chose the option that gave Him the greatest opportunity to demonstrate God's power.

In Luke's account of the healing of the paralytic, Jesus first said to the man, "Son, your sins are forgiven." Immediately, the Pharisees charged Him with blasphemy.

"'Why do you think this is blasphemy? Is it easier to say, "Your sins are forgiven" or "Get up and walk"? I will prove that I, the Son of Man, have the authority on earth to forgive sins.' Then Jesus turned to the paralyzed man and said, 'Stand up, take your mat, and go on home, because you are healed!' And immediately, as everyone watched, the man jumped to his feet, picked up his mat, and went home praising God" (Luke 5:22–25).

Clearly, it was easier for Christ to *say*, "Your sins are forgiven." Anyone could say that, but only Christ could prove that it was true. He did that by choosing the option that was harder to *do*—He healed the paralyzed man. This demonstrated God's power and authority over the earth and brought Him greater glory.

> **HE SPEAKS:** *"I pray that you will begin to understand the incredible greatness of his power for us who believe him. This is the same mighty power that raised Christ from the dead and seated him in the place of honor at God's right hand in the heavenly realms."*
>
> —EPHESIANS 1:19–20

Do you truly believe there is enough power in God's voice to do these kinds of things in your life today? When you consider what the Scriptures demonstrate about His power and authority, don't think of these as exceptions to the rule, rather think of them as examples of what God *can* and *will* do today.

God's voice is powerful, and He wants you to call upon Him expecting to see His greatness revealed. He alone has the authority to accomplish what we need. As you come to recognize the power of God's voice, you will be more willing to seek it, wait for it, and obey it. His voice has the power to keep you from sinking in even the worst of life's storms.

HOW DO YOU KNOW IT'S GOD'S VOICE?

"I know that God is speaking when His voice is so powerful that it comforts, heals, instructs, corrects, and gives wisdom in only a few words. There is a vacuum in my soul that longs for His word in a way that nothing else can satisfy. Hearing Him speak is my spiritual lifeline that keeps my communion with Him fresh. Oh, how I love His voice!"

—PAT ASHLEY

PART FOUR

Discovering God's Plan

"O Lord, you are my light; yes, Lord, you light up my darkness."

—2 SAMUEL 22:29

The script is written. The stage is set. The players are in place.

The instructions of the Divine Director are being made clear as He leads each participant. "Follow the spotlight," He says. "Wherever you see the Light shine, that is where you are supposed to be."

He encourages us not to run stage left when the Light is leading stage right or to dart into center stage when the Light is glowing in the back. Each flicker may not be completely understood, but He encourages us to trust that since He's written the story, He knows what is best.

Obeying these directions not only enables each one to fulfill her personal role as written, but it will help bring others into the Light. When the final curtain descends, what better words could be heard than, "Well done, my good and faithful servant!" (Matthew 25:23).

A Saint Speaks

"The people who are of absolutely no use to God are those who have sat down and have become overgrown with spiritual mildew; all they can do is to refer to an experience they had twenty or thirty years ago. That is of no use whatever; we must be vitally at it all the time. With Paul it was never 'an experience I once had,' but 'the life which I now live.'"

—OSWALD CHAMBERS

11

An Invitational Voice

*"We are God's masterpiece. He has
created us anew in Christ Jesus, so
that we can do the good things he
planned for us long ago."*

—EPHESIANS 2:10

My pastor looked at me across the conference room table and said, "Priscilla, I want you to coordinate the women's conference at our church."

I knew that our church's women's ministry needed to be revitalized. The women seemed to lack enthusiasm for deepening their relationship with the Lord. This became evident as fewer and fewer women participated in programs designed specifically for their spiritual growth. I was thrilled that God would allow me to try to restart the engines of their hearts through a conference that included worship and Bible teaching.

I appointed a committee and started making plans. When word got out to the community, we quickly began to receive calls from women's ministries everywhere, even from other cities and states. My initial reaction was to remain focused on my plan to make the conference just for the women of our church, but the calls kept coming. More and more, it became apparent that women outside our church needed what we were offering.

The committee and I had already spent months planning the event, and we weren't prepared to handle an influx of visitors. But I went back to God in prayer to seek His will. It soon became clear that God's plans and purposes were so much bigger than mine! The conference is four years old now, and each year about four thousand women gather from every denomination to spend a couple of days in the presence of God. The impact of this ministry continues to amaze me. If I had ignored God's plan while stubbornly pursuing my own, my church would have missed a great opportunity to minister to women everywhere. And I wonder how many women might have missed out on a significant encounter with God.

God had already established a designated purpose and plan for the conference long before I was asked to steer it. The question was: "Would I join in with His purposes or stubbornly insist on pursuing my own?" God's kingdom purpose would only be accomplished if I accepted God's invitation to partner with Him to achieve divine success. God has a plan for you too. In every detail of your life, He has predetermined goals for you and desires to reveal them so that you can join Him in yielded obedience to accomplish them. When God allows your spiritual eyes to be open and become aware of His activity on this earth, this is your invitation to join Him in His kingdom agenda for your life and this generation. Seeing God's hand is hearing God's voice.

A SAINT SPEAKS: *"Nothing pleases God more than when we ask for what He wants to give. When we spend time with Him and allow His priorities, passion, and purposes to motivate us, we will ask for things that are closest to His heart."*

—BRUCE WILKINSON

God's Plan for You

The life of Jesus testifies to how the Father invites us to carry out His plans. The beauty of Jesus' life on earth is not that He did His Father's will but that He did His Father's will *and nothing else*. He didn't come up with new ideas or strike out on His own. He understood a principle that we often forget: True success in any endeavor can only come when the Father has initiated the activity and invited our participation.

> **HE SPEAKS:** *"I assure you, the Son can do nothing by himself. He does only what he sees the Father doing. Whatever the Father does, the Son also does."*

—JOHN 5:19

I suspect that the reason we don't often experience the results we want in our endeavors is that we haven't determined to only do what we see the Father doing. We haven't waited for God's invitation. We have invited ourselves to do the things that we want to do in the timing that we want them done, rather than waiting to see what God calls us to.

I have frequently had to ask myself if I *really* want to hear what God's plans are, or if I just want to pursue my own and hope that He will bless them. In looking at my life, I can see how often I've plowed ahead with my own plans hoping God would give them His seal of approval. No wonder some of my plans have fallen flat! They weren't His; they were mine.

Even before you were born, God had an agenda for your career, your finances, and your family. He has a plan for each of us, and as His children, we are to cooperate with it. His plans take precedence over ours.

Our continued prayer should be, *"Lord, open my eyes to see where You are working."* When the indwelling Holy Spirit allows you to see God's movement, you have heard the voice of God. This is His invitation for you to join in and participate. However, accepting God's invitation means that you must be willing to give up your own plans and follow Him. That means always leaving room for God to ask you to do something different —even if it seems frightening or risky.

The truth is—God's invitations are often intimidating but knowing that God is with us will give us the confidence to take on any task. In Ephesians 2:10, Paul reminds us "we are God's masterpiece. He has created us anew in Christ Jesus, so that we can do the good things he planned for us long ago." There are four important parts to this verse that say you are: (1) a masterpiece, (2) created anew, (3) to do good things, and (4) to act according to His plan.

Isn't it exciting to realize that in the eyes of God, we are masterpieces—priceless works of art? He has fully equipped us, through Christ, to carry out His work here on earth. This verse is our assurance that He wants to tell you the plans He has for you and fully equip you to participate in them.

God's Plan in All Things

One day as I prayed during my quiet time, I talked with God about the details of my life. I asked Him to clearly allow me to see His activity throughout the day, so that I could join Him in completing His purposes. As I sat in His presence listening to some melodies from a favorite worship CD, the name of a friend came to mind. She was a dear friend I had been close to, but we had let our lives drift apart when our children came along. I thought of her for a moment and tried to get back to my quiet time. But again, her name came to mind. Thinking that the Lord must have brought her to my attention, I prayed for her and her family. But the Lord's insistent voice continued to speak to me. "Call her. She needs you," He said. The message spoke to my heart and was accompanied by the warm stirring that often accompanies the voice of God.

Prompted by the Spirit, I called her. She answered the phone sounding frustrated and rushed. She explained her husband was at work and her babysitter had called in sick. She was home with her three small children attempting to accomplish the demands of her full-time job that she did from her home office.

That day, my regular quiet time was spent watching my friend's children and folding a mound of clean laundry that was sitting on her couch. She was brought to tears by the thought that God loved her so much that He placed it on the heart of a friend to see to her routine needs.

Peter Lord, whose writing I greatly admire, says, "The worse thing you can do—the quickest way to become insensitive—is to ignore an impression. So you must commit yourself to listening to your Lord for the purpose of responding to what He says, and you must not allow yourself to hear without responding."

When God speaks to your heart or allows you to see Him moving in a different direction than what you had planned, do you respond to Him or turn a deaf ear returning to your own agenda?

As you seek to respond appropriately to God's voice, you must make a decision *today* to be willing to conform your life to God's plan. Be willing to start by looking for His invitations in the daily rhythms of your life. Look for His handiwork while you are doing the mundane duties of your daily routine. Responding to the small invitations will steer you in the right direction for the larger ones.

Deciding now to be willing to refocus your plans is the only way you can willingly and joyfully do what God is asking of you. If you're not prepared to modify your plans, you'll end up missing out on all that God has planned for you.

He invites us to participate in His kingdom agenda, but there's one stipulation: we have to forsake our agenda for His. We can't cling to our own plans and expect to accomplish God's purposes for us. We have to embrace His plans in order to experience His blessings.

Making a decision to adjust your life in obedience to God requires surrender. It means that you make a decision to "wave the white flag" regarding what you want to do and let God accomplish His tasks through you.

God's Plan for You Includes the Church

Since God reveals Himself to us to cause us to participate in His kingdom agenda, a clear way that He speaks to His children is through others who are also participating to accomplish this. God's invitations often come to us through the local church.

When I was growing up, I used to try to get out of helping with household chores any way I could. When I came home from school, tired out from extracurricular activities, I would do my best to be elusive. I hoped that if my parents couldn't see me, they wouldn't ask me to participate. But inevitably my parents would track me down and remind me that I couldn't benefit from the family but not help meet its needs.

The church is the family of God, and it is a means that He uses to speak to His children. Listen carefully: no Christian can accomplish God's complete purpose for their lives without being a part of a local body of believers. Many Christians today desire to partake of the joys of God's family, but they want to "hide out" when it comes to God's plan for building up His body, the church. Some have become comfortable just watching TV evangelists or listening to their favorite preacher on the radio. The problem with this is that it allows you to act like an only child. When you were born again, you were born into a family with siblings. This means that while you're curled up on the couch, you're not helping meet the needs of your Christian family. Christian media is a blessing, but it should never take the place of being connected to your brothers and sisters in Christ.

Although Christians don't need the church in order to have direct access to God, participating in the body of Christ is a vital part of discerning God's voice and responding to His invitation to participate in His plans.

Paul told the Corinthian believers, "All of you together are Christ's body, and each one of you is a separate and necessary part of it" (1 Corinthians 12:27). God has purposefully placed you in the body to help both you and the body do the things that will bring Him glory. As a member of the body of Christ, you have been specifically gifted to accomplish God's purpose for you and the church. This is why your participation in the body of Christ is critical. In order to accomplish God's purposes, you must cooperate by actively sharing your area of gifting within the body.

> **A SAINT SPEAKS:** *"I know the Lord is speaking to me when He confirms things to me through His Word that are already happening around me. Lately God has also used dear friends and the church community around me to speak to my life in a very powerful way and to confirm again what I felt He was saying. When I'm hearing the same theme from a few different sources around me, I know that I need to*

posture my heart to hear Him and not miss where He's leading."

—CHRISTY NOCKELS

Because the members of the church are interconnected, God can and will use other parts of the body to help acquaint you with His leading for your life. When your physical body has a need because of illness or pain, the other parts of your body go into overdrive to try to make up for the problem. Likewise, when the Lord allows you to see a need in your spiritual body, carefully consider if this is God's word to you to respond to that need. When you do this, you will be fulfilling God's purpose for your life, while also participating in His greater kingdom plan.

Not every need you see, however, means that you are the one who needs to meet it. There are many needs within the body and many members to assist in those needs. When God allows you to *see* a need in your local church, or someone brings it to your attention, take this to God for further direction. If God is speaking to you through the church to accomplish His plans, you will notice a pattern in your Bible study, prayer, and your circumstances that will all point you in the same direction. God has a specific plan for your life; wait and join in on only those in which He invites you to participate.

HE SPEAKS: *"Let us not neglect our meeting together, as some people do, but encourage and warn each other, especially now that the day of his coming back again is drawing near."*

—HEBREWS 10:25

My aunt Elizabeth, who has been our church's children's ministry leader for twenty-five years, asked me to come down and give the younger children their Sunday school lesson. My parents had a flannel board and biblical characters they used to tell Bible stories, and I always enjoyed taking it to my room to tell my imaginary class a story. So I was glad to help at church and spent long hours trying to figure out how I could tell the story in a way that would be appealing to the children.

I don't remember all of the details—although I do recall something about water balloons! The kids were very excited and learned a lot from the lesson. After that my aunt sensed that I was to be a regular part of that ministry. She thought that God wanted to use a younger person, like me, to invigorate the Sunday school lessons and get the kids excited about God's Word. Although I didn't realize it at the time, this was God's way of using the church to confirm His will for me. The body was in need. He had gifted me to accomplish the task and given me a heart that was willing.

God arranges all our circumstances and enables us to see Him moving in them as a way of inviting us to participate. This means that when you're seeking to discern God's voice, you must at least be *aware* of what God is doing within the body of Christ and consider how it might apply to you individually.

> **HE SPEAKS:** *"We can make our plans, but the Lord determines our steps."*
>
> —PROVERBS 16:9

When you hear God's inviting voice within the church, you may feel the Holy Spirit nudging you to do something you don't feel equipped to do. *If God calls you, believe that He has already equipped you to do it.* You're a masterpiece, remember? Respond in obedience and give Him the opportunity to display His supernatural power in your life as He uses you for His purposes and His glory. A heavenly invitation has been written and sent to you. Open it. Read it and accept it.

HOW DO YOU KNOW IT'S GOD'S VOICE?

"There are times when God just drops something into my mind—and I know it is Him. I know that I know—so much so that even if there's resistance to what I believe I am to do, I know I have to do it. This is what happened when God laid it on my heart thirty some years ago to write the 'Precept Upon Precept Bible' studies. I had to do it—and I knew it. Time has proven it to be of God."

—KAY ARTHUR

12

A Timely Voice

"The Lord isn't slow about keeping his promises, as some people think he is."

—2 PETER 3:9 (CEV)

All week long I had reminded Jerry that our yearly garage sale was on Friday. Every day I asked if we could park one of our two cars outside of the garage, so we could start moving in the things we were planning to sell. I didn't want to wait until the last minute. I knew we needed to do the job a little at a time to keep it from overwhelming us.

But that week, Jerry was so swamped with other things that he didn't even say, much less do, anything about the garage sale. He was silent and distant. He didn't give me the okay to store sale items in his garage space, nor did he begin to move the large items downstairs. All I could do was wait until he could help me.

Now, here it was Thursday night. The garage sale was to begin promptly at 7:00 the next morning. But after a long day working and then mowing the lawn in the late afternoon, Jerry had gone into our bedroom to rest. Trying my best not to badger him, I did what I could. I pulled out the smaller items we planned to sell and put them in the living room.

Jerry resurfaced around 9:00 PM and began to help. It was very clear that he wasn't at all happy about having to work so late in the evening. As he huffed and sighed, I squelched the deep desire to yell, "I told you not to wait until the last minute!"

For a month I had been creating a list of the items that were too big for me to get by myself. When he saw the long list, he declared emphatically, "I'm tired!"

Now we were both frustrated!

God never looks at the list of important life circumstances that we need His help with and says, "I'm tired!" If He sometimes seems silent, His inactivity isn't based on His lack of energy or interest. The answer for His silence may be found in this simple truth: God's timing may not coincide with ours. But just as He has specific plans for our life, we must confidently believe that He also has specific timing. He orchestrates not only the events in your life, but the timing in which they occur. He will speak when everything is in place for Him to reveal the next steps for our life.

Trusting God's Timing

Elizabeth and Zachariah wanted a child (Luke 1). But though they had prayed for one for years, God had never blessed them. It wasn't until they were very old that an angel appeared to Zechariah and told him, "God has heard your prayer, and your wife, Elizabeth, will bear you a son!" (v. 13). This child, John, was to have a special mission. He was going to prepare the people for the birth of Jesus. There was more at stake than just giving a couple the child they longed for. God had a much greater plan, and the time was ripe for it to be fulfilled. Elizabeth wasn't too old to be a mother. And God hadn't spoken too late. He had waited until everything was in place for the birth of His Son and then gave clear, powerful instructions to those involved.

I admit that I've often questioned God's timing. When I needed clarity on a specific circumstance, yet felt that He wasn't providing it, I sulked.

But time and again the Lord has shown me that the reason He chose to wait to reveal something concerning His will for my life, is because I would have most assuredly tried to rush ahead of God rather than wait for Him. If He had spoken to me five years ago about the details of the ministry He has entrusted to me now, I would either have rushed impatiently toward it, before I was emotionally and spiritually equipped for the demands, or run away in fear. Knowing this, the Father wisely chose to show me just what I need to know. The timing of God's message to us is just as important as the message itself. And when the time is right for us to know, we will.

> **A SAINT SPEAKS:** *"We must also understand that sometimes the silence of the Lord is His way of letting us grow, just as a mother allows her child to fall and get up again when he is learning to walk."*
>
> —CORRIE TEN BOOM

The True Guide

John 16:13 paints the picture of the Holy Spirit as our "guide." The term used actually means *to guide while one is on one's way.* The mental image is of one who gives continuous direction on a need-to-know basis. Much of the heartache and frustration I have encountered in discerning God's voice came because I wanted direction before God was ready to give it. I wasn't willing to trust God's timing in revealing His plans for me.

When I traveled to the Holy Land several years ago, my goal was to see and learn as much biblical history as I could. How grateful I was that our tour guide didn't download all the information about the places we were going to and then leave me to my own devices. Rather, the learned Jewish scholar walked with us each step of the way. At each destination, he told us all about the location and the many things we needed to know. Then he took us on to our next location. Getting our information as we went, helped us to get the most value from our trip.

As your guide the Holy Spirit doesn't give you all the directions up front and then leave you alone either. He tells you what you need to know for now and then updates His instructions as you step out in faith and obedience.

God told David, "I will counsel you with My eye upon you" (Psalm 32:8 NASB). He wanted the psalmist to understand that He wouldn't just give His direction once and then not follow up. God gives specific, ongoing direction to those closest to Him. He stands nearby, watching every career move, every relational endeavor, and every financial decision. He sees every step and anticipates every mishap. He knows when He will need to catch you even before you fall. Just as I stand near my precious little one, constantly anticipating how I should assist him to get to his desired destination, He is standing close by you, ready to give you His counsel, hold your hand, and steady you.

God will use the appropriate means necessary to reveal His will in His timing. When it is time for you and me to know, we will. If you have not yet heard from God on a particular issue, it is not because God doesn't know how to reach you. It may be because He doesn't want to give you clarity yet. Don't try to make your time constraints God's.

Jesus expressed this to the disciples when He said, "I have many more things to say to you, but you cannot bear them now" (John 16:12 NASB). There is a time for everything. Until you know plainly what to do next, keep obediently doing what you are sure of.

When airplanes land, their individual flight pattern is not all that matters. The air-traffic controller must consider the other planes in the air and waiting for take off. He needs to know how each will be affected by the landing directions that are given. The timing of when the pilot receives the next set of instructions depends on all the planes that are in the air. Before receiving instructions from the control tower, the pilot doesn't say, "I'm going to start landing my plane." Doing so could be detrimental to him, his passengers, and all the other planes. He will wait for directions from someone who can see more than he can from his limited perspective.

When God gives you instructions, trust that He has given you everything you need *now*. When the time is right, He will give you more. Moving forward before you hear from God could be extremely detrimental to you and all that God has planned.

> **HE SPEAKS:** *"There is a time for everything, a season for every activity under heaven. A time to be quiet and a time to speak up."*
>
> —ECCLESIASTES 3:1, 7

God's Truth Is Freely Given

Paul addresses the timeliness of God's word to us in 1 Corinthians 2:12 (NASB). He says that we have been given the Spirit of God, so that "we may know the things freely given to us by God." The things the Spirit freely gives us are the things we need to know *now*. Much of the frustration we feel about hearing God's voice and knowing His will is the result of wanting what isn't freely given. When we pray, *Lord, show me your will,* we are often asking for truth that isn't pertinent until twenty years from now. We want God to paint the whole picture for us right away. But Jesus said to the disciples, "There is so much more I want to tell you, but you can't bear it now" (John 16:12).

We need to be clear about what Jesus meant when He said this. He didn't mean that God withholds truth from some of His children and entrusts others with special knowledge. God doesn't play favorites. He promises that the Holy Spirit will lead us into *all* truth (John 16:13). Jesus wasn't trying to hide something from His disciples, and He isn't trying to hide anything from us. What He was saying was that He can't give us the truth all at once because He knows we can't handle it all at once. God's truth will be given to us right on time!

> **A SAINT SPEAKS:** *"The thief's voice, unlike God's voice, threatens and intimidates on the basis of fear: 'If you don't do this, you'll be sorry.' It may order you or try to force you*

to do things. It is often urgent and pressing, sermonizing and demeaning: Do this now! If you wait all will be lost!"

—JAN JOHNSON

No Need to Hurry

If we truly believe that God will speak in the appropriate time, we should never feel hurried or pressured about making decisions that are not rooted in a deep-seated internal peace. If you are not clear, do not move. Only when God has spoken will you be cued to respond in obedience. His purposes have been specifically calculated with you in mind. Nothing takes God off guard. Remember, His plan for you began at the beginning of time. When we feel rushed and hurried to make a decision that is not firmly planted on God's Word, God is probably not the one speaking. Nowhere in Scripture does God tell anyone to rush into a decision. On the contrary, He patiently and persistently gives us clarity before requiring obedience. If you feel an overwhelming urge to act spontaneously, pull in the reins. God only asks for an immediate response once His will is clearly revealed.

A friend of mine, who was a financially struggling seminary student, wanted to purchase a new car. A pushy salesman was trying to rush her into a decision. The deal that the salesman was giving her was a good one, but she felt uneasy and uncertain. Even though she knew she might miss out on the deal, she felt anxious about making such a huge financial decision on the spot. Wisely, she walked away from the offer. Two weeks later she was blessed with a free car from an anonymous donor.

If you do not feel assurance in decisions you are making, stop and listen for the voice of the Holy Spirit to guide you. God's voice is timely. He is not behind schedule and will not cause you to miss out on His will. As you wait for God to speak and fulfill His word to you, just stand firm in your faith, trust Him to guide you one step at a time, and then follow wherever He leads.

Wait in Silence

Waiting for God to bring clarity can be difficult. In chapter 1, we talked about the prophet Habakkuk and how frustrated he became while waiting for God's direction (Habakkuk 1–2). Do you remember where Habakkuk said he was going to wait to hear from God? On the watchtower. This is very important. The watchtower was always positioned well above the ground in order to provide a view for miles around. It gave the guard in the tower a completely different view of his circumstances.

Habakkuk had to climb above the ground level of his life in order to focus his eyes on God and tune his ears to hear His voice. As we wait for God to speak or to fulfill His word to us, we too must wait on the watchtower. We have to leave our problems on the ground level, focus our attention completely on God, and wait.

> **A SAINT SPEAKS:** *"If you told God on your knees that you had reached an impasse, were handing it over to him then leave it with him. Do not go to the first Christian you meet and say, 'You know, I have an awful problem; I don't know what to do.' Don't discuss it. Leave it with God and go on the watchtower."*
>
> —D. Martyn Lloyd-Jones

Waiting on the watchtower means waiting in silence. It means tuning out the world around you and purposefully focusing them on God. But, oh, how we dread silence! We're often so afraid of it that we decide to stay on "ground level" and fill the void with some kind of busy, noisy activity. We find it even more unbearable when we know that God is right there with us, but choosing not to speak.

While we're waiting on the watchtower, Satan finds ways to make us question God's love for us. We wonder if He has forgotten us because we aren't important enough. We fear that He may not be speaking or moving because we haven't made a big enough impression on Him. We find ourselves feeling the need to work harder to please Him, so we can in some way capture His attention.

Friend, don't let Satan deceive you in this way. The Lord's decision to allow the silence has nothing to do with who you are or where you are on your spiritual journey. He doesn't respond only to those we consider the "spiritual elite." He responds to us all—young and old, black and white, tall and short, fat and skinny. He even responds to those of us who aren't living a life of complete submission to Him. He is no respecter of persons, and His prejudices are not the prejudices of man. His only bias is against our sin.

There are reasons for God's silence. It may be He wants to strengthen our relationship with Him by building our trust in Him. His silence teaches us to let go of the need for control that often blinds us to His ability to reign in every situation. When we know we aren't in control, our only option is to place ourselves completely in His hands. There's something in the silence we would miss if He spoke to us just now—the special trust that comes when we know we don't know everything.

> **A SAINT SPEAKS:** *"My acceptance of His timing was a rigorous exercise in trust. I was tempted to charge the Lord with negligence and inattention, like the disciples in the boat in a storm. They toiled frantically until the situation became impossible and then instead of asking for Jesus' help they yelled, 'Master, don't you care that we're drowning?' They weren't perishing; they were panicking. It was not too late. Jesus got up and merely spoke to the wind and sea."*
>
> —ELISABETH ELLIOT

It isn't necessary for us to know the entire game plan as long as we trust the One who does. Our heavenly Father doesn't give us all of the answers at once. Sometimes He just watches and waits to see if we will simply obey His command to "be silent, and know that I am God!" (Psalm 46:10).

Is God only God when we hear Him speaking or see Him moving?

Or we will still trust that He is still our Father, even if we hear no voice from heaven and see nothing happening? Whether or not He is responding in the way we would prefer is of no consequence. We must believe that He is working on our behalf even when He chooses not to say a single word. In His silence, He speaks volumes to us. He commands us to wait on Him and focus our attention on His holiness.

Are you calling out to the silent Jesus right now for the solution to a problem you face? Are you sitting on the watchtower? He is asking you to trust Him until the time for His plan is ripe. Simply trust!

> **HE SPEAKS:** *"Wait on the Lord; be of good courage, and He shall strengthen your heart; wait, I say, on the Lord."*
>
> —PSALM 27:14 (NKJV)

Trust God's Timing

Our life is like a box containing all the pieces of a giant jigsaw puzzle, and only God can see the picture on the lid. He sees the entire layout and knows just how and when all the pieces need to come together. We can be certain that God knows exactly the right time to speak and act.

Often what you sense the Spirit saying to you will seem puzzling. That's because there's a heavenly agenda to every situation that only the Spirit can see. There's a depth of truth about a person, a situation, or a problem that neither you nor anyone else can access through human wisdom. The Holy Spirit will wait to reveal these deep truths to you until you're ready to understand and accept them. If He revealed them before you're ready, they could overwhelm you.

If we believe that God will speak and act in a timely way, we can be still and wait on the Lord. What a relief! This gives us courage and strengthens our heart. Knowing that God promises to fulfill His own word, we don't have to be anxious for anything—not a mate, financial assistance, a ministry opportunity, career advancement, or even just His direction. Waiting on the Lord's timing frees us from the burden of trying to make things happen. Trust Him to guide you one step at a time, and then follow wherever He leads.

HOW DO YOU KNOW IT'S GOD'S VOICE?

"I know the Lord is speaking when I cannot rest. Yes, I know that sounds negative, but there have been times when His will has not been very clear to me. The Lord seems to put restlessness in my heart that just won't go away until I stop and ask Him, 'What Lord; what is it?' I do believe that is why the Lord Jesus told us to abide in Him. Oh, that we would learn to abide and follow Him wherever He leads!"

—DAMARIS CARBAUGH

13

A Fatherly Voice

"See how very much our heavenly Father loves us for he allows us to be called his children, and we really are!"

—1 JOHN 3:1

My father is a great dad, but sometimes he has trouble remembering my name. When I was young, he couldn't quite figure out which of his four children I was. He would call Anthony, Jonathan, and Chrystal in quick succession before he finally settled on Priscilla. The four of us got used to hearing this spill of names. We would anxiously wait for the fourth name to escape his lips, knowing that this was the person he wanted to speak to. To this day my father will often call my sister or me "Crissilla." That's the name that comes out when he begins to call one of us but realizes halfway through that he really wants to speak to the other.

Our heavenly Father doesn't have this problem. He isn't frantically searching for our name, and He doesn't get us confused with all His other kids. He knows just who we are and He has a personal message just for us. Even if we sometimes stumble and disappoint Him, He speaks in a way any loving father would. He convicts and corrects us, but He never condemns. Our loving Father is always there ready to offer forgiveness when we humbly repent from our sins. Let's look at some Scriptures that demonstrate how our Father loves us and calls us by name to do His will.

> **GOD SPEAKS:** *"I will give you treasures hidden in the darkness—secret riches. I will do this so you may know that I am the Lord, the God of Israel, the one who calls you by name."*
>
> —Isaiah 45:3

A Personal Message

When God wanted to speak to a confused little boy ministering in His temple, He called him by name: "Samuel! Samuel!" (1 Samuel 3:10). When He wanted to get the attention of a weeping woman seeking the body of her crucified Lord, He called her by name: "Mary!" (John 20:16). When He wanted to save a man traveling to Damascus to persecute Christians, He called him by name: "Saul! Saul!" (Acts 9:4). Often, when God spoke to biblical characters, He used their names. This shows us that God is in to speaking to His children personally.

Today, God does this through the Holy Spirit. God's desire to lead you personally means two things: First, no matter what stage of your Christian life you are in (fledgling believer or seasoned Christian), God will speak in a way that you can hear and understand Him. Second, since His personalized messages will be designed to direct you in His will for *your* life, it is important that we do not hold others accountable for what God is speaking to us. He is your guide on your life journey, and His instructions for you have your name on them.

Michelle is one of the godliest women I know. She has an intimate relationship with the Lord and listens intently to hear the Holy Spirit, so He can steer her choices. Because of her personal convictions, she follows a code of conduct that many would consider unnecessarily rigid. She avoids many movies, books, and television shows because of her personal convictions. Whenever a few of us are hanging out together and decide to do something that, while not sinful, goes against what she feels is right for her, she parts company with a smile on her face. She doesn't try to impose her convictions on us or try to get us to change our plans to suit her. She just responds obediently to God's personal leading in her life.

When we know that God is requiring us to do a certain thing, it can be easy for us to assume that He must be requiring everyone else to do the same thing. If we think this way, we run the risk of becoming legalistic and placing other believers in bondage.

There are some "black-and-white" areas of life in which Scripture gives clear instruction that all believers must obey. And if God's Word takes a clear stand on an issue you're facing, don't waste your time praying and fasting about it. The Holy Spirit will never speak contrary to what is written. However, there are some areas where the Scriptures give general guidelines but may not expressly address a question or situation you are facing. These are areas where we need God's specific, personal guidance. When deciding what church you should join, where you should live, whether you should marry or stay single, or even something as simple as what type of entertainment you can enjoy, ask the Spirit for His specific guidance. God cares about the details of your life. He is eager to tell you whether what you want to do is right or wrong. He will give you a personal conviction about these matters (Romans 14:4–5).

The Father knows the plans He has for your life, and He will direct you personally based on what He wants you to accomplish. For the woman who is called to be a full-time mom, He may give a personal conviction about working outside of the home. For the woman directed to lead a Bible study, He may give a conviction about the amount of time she chooses to spend in preparation. The woman God leads to homeschool will be guided by the Holy Spirit to steer clear of traditional means of schooling. All of these promptings by God are specifically designed for each woman to foster her needs and the needs of her loved ones.

HE SPEAKS: *"Do not let what is for you a good thing be spoken of as evil."*

—ROMANS 14:16 (NASB)

Same Destination, Different Directions

The main road to downtown Dallas from where I live is north on Highway 35. I think it is the most efficient and obvious way for anyone to go to downtown. But there are many people who choose another route. Although I do tend to think that my directions are the best, it doesn't mean this is the only way to go. These directions work for me, but another way may be best for someone else's journey.

As God leads us in our journey toward Him, there are different avenues for each of us. The Holy Spirit draws an individual map for us to follow. Others may not choose our road, and they shouldn't if it is not a part of the map they have been given. We shouldn't challenge them regarding their chosen route, as long as their actions fall within the guidelines of Scripture. Each person should be following the Lord in obedience in a way that brings glory to God. Our responsibility is not to judge but only to be sure we are following God's leading in our own lives.

We should enjoy the things that the Lord has given us the freedom to enjoy and not feel bad if God has restricted the freedom of others in those same areas. By the same token, we should be careful to allow others the freedom to do what He is asking of them, even if He has restricted us in that same area. You are accountable to the Lord for what He personally requires of you. James 4:17 (NASB) tells us, "To one who knows the right thing to do and does not do it, to him it is sin."

When the Holy Spirit gives you His specific insight for you, and you recognize that leading but then deliberately go against it, you sin against God. This is true even if the issue is something as seemingly trivial as eating more than you should, taking a particular job, wearing a certain outfit, or shopping at your favorite outlet store. If the Holy Spirit is clearly leading you to do something—or to refrain from doing it—yield to His personal word in your life. It's your loving Father's way of calling you by name in an effort to move you toward His desired destination for you.

God always works in a way that leads us forward. If the message you are hearing is one that condemns you and stops you from accomplishing His will, it isn't the voice of God you are hearing. It is the voice of the Enemy.

A SAINT SPEAKS: *"'I am someone God so loves' is a message we're likely to hear from God in contemplation. God is so anxious to tell us this that the only time God is pictured in a hurry in Scripture is when the father ran down the trail to the prodigal son, 'threw his arms around him and kissed him.'"*

—JAN JOHNSON

A Loving Message

When I went off to college, I left the sheltered life of my Christian family, school, and friends and entered another world. I was excited by the prospect of my new, independent lifestyle. However, I soon found myself living in a way that I knew wasn't pleasing to the Lord. As a result, I later struggled with condemning thoughts about some of the things I had done during my undergraduate education.

No matter what I accomplished or how far I removed myself from the bad choices of the past, a nagging voice inside my head kept pouring on the guilt. I wondered why God would continually remind me about my past. Though I had sought God's forgiveness, I couldn't seem to forgive myself and erase these thoughts from my mind.

As I struggled with this I ran across a verse that spoke to my heart: "I—yes, I alone—am the one who blots out your sins for my own sake and will never think of them again" (Isaiah 43:25).

With these loving words, the Lord quickly reminded me that His goal is never to bring guilt and condemnation by continually reminding me of the sins of my past, rather He desires to bring healing and restoration by forgiving my sin and throwing it into the sea of forgetfulness. God's desires is to always lovingly direct us to His grace.

As God's character is revealed in Scripture, we see in 1 John 4:8, "God is love." Love is who He is and what He invites us to experience. When God speaks to us, He doesn't point out our sin to condemn us or burden us with guilt. His desire is to lovingly reveal our sin and encourage us to confess it, so He can cleanse and change us. He never wants us to act out of guilt or fear of rejection but rather out of a love relationship with Him.

> **A SAINT SPEAKS:** *"The purpose of the voice of condemnation is to push you away from His presence—that which is the very source of your victory. The purpose of the voice of conviction is to press you into the face of Christ."*
>
> —BOB SORGE

There's a difference between God's *convicting* voice and the Enemy's *condemning* voice. *Condemn* means to consider something worthy of punishment. *Convict* means to bring something to light in order to correct it. The Enemy's voice causes us to feel guilt and offers no clear means of relief. But when the Spirit convicts us of sin, He always provides a road map out and away from sin. In Him, there is no condemnation (Romans 8:1).

No Condemnation

John 8 tells us about some Pharisees who caught a woman in the very act of adultery. They dragged her into the temple where Jesus was teaching and publicly exposed her sin. How must she have felt? Imagine someone catching you in some sinful act and dragging you to a Bible study at your church where all of your friends are gathered! It might not have been quite so bad if these men had been trying to restore the woman. But that had nothing to do with it. They just wanted to expose, embarrass, and disgrace her. That's Satan's goal as well. You can know the voice of the Enemy when what you hear is clearly meant to disgrace you.

> **HE SPEAKS:** *"Fear not, for you will not be put to shame; and do not feel humiliated, for you will not be disgraced; but you will forget the shame of your youth, and the reproach of your widowhood you will remember no more."*
>
> —ISAIAH 54:4 (NASB)

The Pharisees also wanted to discredit Jesus, so they reminded Him that the law said that such women were supposed to be stoned. Then they demanded to know what He planned to do about it. "All right, stone her," Jesus said. "But let those who have never sinned throw the first stones!" (John 8:7). The Pharisees quickly realized that they didn't qualify, and one by one they walked out.

The only one who had the right to throw a stone was the One speaking. Yet, He did not throw the stone. Listen to that again: *He did not throw the stone*. Friend, always remember that great truth. God has the right to condemn us because He is without sin, but He has chosen to bestow grace on us despite what we have done. This is because His very nature is love.

When the Pharisees were gone, Jesus spoke to the woman.

"Where are your accusers? "Didn't even one of them condemn you?"
"No, Lord," she said.
And Jesus said, "Neither do I. Go and sin no more" (vv. 10–11).

Jesus didn't ignore the woman's sin or make excuses for it; He just didn't condemn her for it. God's voice will *convict* us (point out our sin), but it will also express His love for us. It won't *condemn* us or burden us with guilt. It will offer us grace to leave the sin behind and continue on in righteousness.

Whenever I feel the pain of "stones" thrown at me, I quickly realize they didn't come from my loving Father. For instance, if I miss my quiet time and begin to feel guilty, I recognize this isn't the voice of the Lord that I'm hearing. God desires for me to know Him and spend time with Him. But His way of wooing me back to Him is to fill me with a homesick longing to come to Him out of love and affection.

According to Revelation 12:10 (NASB), it is the Enemy that seeks to "accuse [the believer] before our God day and night." If you are struggling because you are feeling condemned, take time right now to pray. If you have never asked God to forgive you for this sin, ask Him now. But if you have already received God's forgiveness, tell Him that you now recognize that these words of condemnation are not from Him. Ask Him to remove these feelings of guilt and let you hear His voice, not the Enemy's.

> **HE SPEAKS:** *"There is no condemnation for those who belong to Christ Jesus."*
>
> —ROMANS 8:1

Christ bore the punishment for your sin once and for all on the cross. Therefore, when God speaks to you now, His words won't dispense judgment. They may reveal your shortcomings so you'll recognize your sins, but He will buffer this revelation with His grace, love, and another chance. While condemnation points out the problem only to judge you and make you feel guilty, God's soothing words of conviction offer you a solution. You'll know your heavenly Father's voice by its loving tone.

When determining whether or not you are hearing from God, always consider the "Fatherliness" of God, as it is revealed in His Word. Remember that the New Testament paints a picture of One who loved you so much that He gave the life of His only Son, so that there would be no separation between you. His entire goal, since the beginning of time, is to have a personal, intimate, loving fellowship between the two of you. If what you hear jeopardizes the character of our Abba Father, then know with full assurance that the voice is not God's.

Is the loving Father calling your name? Draw near to Him and like Samuel answer, "Speak, Lord, for your servant is listening."

HOW DO YOU KNOW IT'S GOD'S VOICE?

"I know God is speaking to me when I am awakened during the night and it's difficult to get back to sleep. I try not to second-guess my sudden state of awakening . . . whether I was nudged by God or something I ate before bed. I just lie there and talk to God. I talk openly and honestly to Him. I tell Him how much I love Him. If I have anything that concerns me, I present my requests to Him. I know He is ready to set my mind at ease, so I talk to Him about anything that weighs on my heart and mind. I have the assurance that no matter what time of day or night, God is as close to me as my prayers."

—BABBIE MASON

14

A Challenging Voice

*"The gate is narrow and the way is
hard, that leads to life."*

—MATTHEW 7:14 (ESV)

My son looked intently at the cocoon that hung on the limb of the bush behind our house. For days, he'd been watching the tiny structure as I tried to use the opportunity to teach him a little about nature. He'd been eagerly waiting for the day when the emperor moth I had told him about would finally emerge. Today seemed to be the day. The little cocoon rocked and shook as we watch the tiny insect struggle to free itself from the confines of the shell. Frustrated by the hours of waiting, my son begged me to assist the moth in making its exit. I tried my best to share a profound lesson with a two-year-old—a lesson that the Lord used to penetrate my heart even as I spoke it. "The moth has to struggle in order to reach its full potential," I told him. "If the moth escapes prematurely from the cocoon, it will be crippled for the rest of its life. It is only as it takes on the challenge of battling its way out of the cocoon that its full wingspan and leg strength are developed."

Since our heavenly Father's greatest goal is for us to grow into our full spiritual potential, we will often be challenged by the things He calls us to do. His word may alarm or even frighten us, because we know that there is no way we can do what He is asking in our own power. But God's purposes are always higher than ours. When we follow His will in obedience, His word will cause us to step away from the comfort zone of our natural abilities and step into the realm of His supernatural possibilities. You will recognize God's voice when His plans challenge you.

A Challenging Message

Our heavenly Father knows that we need to stretch in order to grow spiritually. So when He speaks, I often find that His messages challenge me. Since His ways are not our ways and His thoughts are not our thoughts (Isaiah 55:8 NASB), I find that most frequently His messages not only go beyond my natural thought processes, but they also exceed my natural abilities. Messages like this make me uncomfortable because I know there's no way I can do what God is asking in my own power.

When God called Jeremiah to be His spokesman, the young man protested that the job would be too much for him. "I can't speak for you!" he protested. "I'm too young!" (Jeremiah 1:6). He was afraid to accept God's challenging assignment.

"'Don't say that,' the Lord replied, 'for you must go wherever I send you and say whatever I tell you. And don't be afraid of the people, for I will be with you and take care of you. I, the Lord, have spoken!'" (vv. 7–8).

Jeremiah accepted God's challenge, stepped out in obedience, and proclaimed the words God put in his mouth. He told the people of Judah exactly what would happen to them if they didn't repent of their sins and turn back to God: the Babylonians would destroy Jerusalem and carry them into captivity.

As a result of his message, the Jews beat Jeremiah and put him in prison on several occasions. Although Jeremiah was naturally timid, God gave him the courage to persevere in the face of persecution, and he spoke God's messages for more than forty years.

Accepting God's challenge is often hard for me in my own speaking ministry. After seeking the Lord and preparing a message, I feel I know what my audience needs to hear, and I travel to an engagement sure of what my message will be. However, I never tell anyone ahead of time what I will be talking about. That's because once a conference gets underway, the Lord often impresses on me the need to address an entirely different topic. Hours, or sometimes minutes, before I am to speak, I sense God leading me in another direction based on what He is doing at the event.

This is always a scary and uncomfortable place to be! It would be so much easier for me to just go ahead and give the talk I've prepared. But since I know that God's power and anointing will only accompany *His* message, I know that I have to let go of my words and allow God to speak through me. As I do, God gives me the courage and power I need to proclaim His message.

> **A SAINT SPEAKS:** *"Have you ever heard the Master say something very difficult to you? If you haven't, I question whether you have ever heard Him say anything at all."*
>
> —OSWALD CHAMBERS

It's often tempting to do the opposite of what God asks simply because it would be easier. But doing the easier thing will never stretch you by forcing you to tap into your divine resources. God wants to help you to grow by allowing you to see what He can do when you admit you can't. While a sense of your own weakness will help keep you humble before God, you shouldn't use it as an excuse for not doing what God calls you to do.

His Strength through Our Weakness

Throughout the Bible we see many instances of people whom God called from unlikely places asking them to do things that were far beyond their abilities and what they felt equipped to do. In fact, this seems to be the most consistent way to characterize God's voice in Scripture. When He spoke:

- Noah was asked to build an ark.

- Abraham was asked to leave his home for an unknown country.

- Esther was asked to plead the case for her people before a king.

- Gideon was asked to go to battle with less than adequate troops.

- Samuel was asked to give a tough message to his mentor.

- Mary was asked to become the mother of the Messiah.

The outstanding accomplishments of Moses' life began with a challenging message from God. Earlier, we recalled the remarkable things that God did to advance His kingdom when Moses surrendered his plans and joined in with God's. But when Moses first heard God's plan for him, he didn't start off saying, "Sure, God. No problem." Instead he was overwhelmed by what God was asking him to do. When God called Moses to be His spokesman, Moses protested, saying, "I can't do it! I'm no orator. Why should Pharaoh listen to me?" (Exodus 6:30). He was afraid to accept God's challenging assignment. But then God said to Moses, "Pay close attention to this. I will make you seem like God to Pharaoh" (Exodus 7:1).

Can you imagine how Moses must have felt when he heard God say he would make him seem like God Himself! In other words, God wanted to supernaturally equip Moses for the task and allow the power of the Almighty to be manifested through him. Likewise, when we willingly submit to God's challenges despite our hesitancy, we are releasing the splendors of the Almighty to be seen in us.

If you know God is speaking to you, but the task seems too big, trust God to take care of the details. He isn't expecting you to pull this off in your own ability. He's waiting for you to just say yes and then get out of His way. It is through your *inability* that He reveals His power.

When I look back at the progression that God has taken me on in ministry, every stage of it has been built on a challenging message from God. Most often I have been afraid and intimidated by the thing the Lord has presented for me to do. However, I have learned that the mere fact that a situation brings something that I know I am unable to accomplish in my own power is often my cue to move forward, so that God can be seen in me. As I have sought Him, God has always showed up—just in time—to give me what I need.

In 2 Corinthians 12:9, Paul talks about his feelings of inadequacy and his experience with how God worked supernaturally through him. Each time he felt ill-equipped to take on the challenge that God was asking of him, God reminded him He had already provided all that he needed. "Each time he [God] said, 'My gracious favor is all you need. My power works best in your weakness.' So now I am glad to boast about my weaknesses, so that the power of Christ may work through me."

Friend, it is a sure thing, God will provide where He guides. It is better for you to choose the more challenging road, if God is in it, than to select the route that is easier and more convenient, but lacks the presence and power of God.

> **A SAINT SPEAKS:** *"I love Jesus and have been enjoying a relationship with Him for almost 35 years, but my stubborn Italian flesh still collides with God's perfect will for my life. How I yearn to arrive at a place when my consistent response to the Lord's voice will be that of Jesus: 'Not my will Lord, but Yours.'"*
>
> —ELLIE LOFARO

Inevitably, the voice of the Enemy or the voice of your own ego will present a more comfortable alternative for you to choose. It's often tempting to do the opposite of what God asks simply because it would be easier. But doing the easier thing will never stretch you by forcing you to tap into your divine resources. Satan's primary goal is to keep us in the comfortable cocoons that keep us from growing into the people God intends for us to be. The Enemy will never ask you to step outside your comfort zone because he doesn't want you to experience the fullness of God's power. Your own ego will never ask you to do anything that may cause you embarrassment or a blow to your self-image. Your Father, on the other hand, wants to help you grow by allowing you to see what He can do when you admit you can't. It is only when we walk in faith, and trust Him to provide what we cannot do ourselves that His glory and majesty is displayed.

When Henry Blackaby, author of *Experiencing God*, was still in seminary, his church asked him to be the music and education director. Since he had never sung in a choir nor led music, he didn't feel equipped to take this responsibility. But as he continued to seek the Lord's will, he felt God was leading him to respond. Despite his inexperience, he willingly obeyed. He successfully served in this capacity for two years, and then the church called him to be their pastor. Even though he hadn't preached many sermons, he agreed. Today he has blessed millions of people through his ministry and his books—all because he obediently responded to God's plan for his life.

Have you at times felt tempted to walk away from what you know God is asking you to do because it just seemed too hard? God is waiting to bring you into His will and do wondrous things through you. *Most often it will be tempting to do the opposite of what God is asking, because that option will be easier.* But distinguishing God's voice from all others can often be determined when we set out to choose the option that will cause God's power to be seen.

> **A SAINT SPEAKS:** *"One of the ways we know His voice is that its content is such that He keeps us at a point of trusting Him for something new—in ourselves, in our loved ones, in our ministry. Trusting Him for deeper levels. For more growth. For wider usage. And always advancing from faith to faith."*
>
> —PETER LORD

The Hard Road

When I started desiring to clearly hear God's voice, it occurred to me that I was often hesitant to hear what He had to say because of the challenge it might bring. I didn't want Him asking me to do things I didn't want to do. What if He asked me to pack up my family and be a missionary in some desolate place? What if He wanted me to stay in a job I couldn't stand? What if He wanted me to stay single? I assume that you've had these same kinds of questions at some point.

Don't confuse understanding God's will with agreeing with it. We won't always immediately agree with everything God allows us to understand. God had to remind me of who He is: *He is love* and *He is good*. These are not mere personality traits of God. They are innate in the very person of God. Knowing this assures me that He will ask me to do only what is best for me and that, although I won't always agree with Him initially, I can trust His plan for me. And you can trust His plan for you. God desires to show His strength through you and will encourage you to do things that require you to trust and have faith in His work in you. The Enemy's voice will tell you, "You don't have enough. You are not able. You can't." The voice of the Spirit says, "I have enough. I am able. I can!"

Today, choose not to fear God's challenging voice and the plans He has for you. Instead, prepare to obey and walk in the fullness of the supernatural abundant life that He has called you to live.

HOW DO YOU KNOW IT'S GOD'S VOICE?

"I know the Lord is speaking to me when the voice I hear is always challenging, always convicting, and never allows me to be comfortable where I am. Not having a father, what an honor it is to have One who loves me so much that His greatest desire is to see me grow."

—KIRK FRANKLIN

PART : FIVE

Responding to God's Voice

"Everyone who hears these words of mine and puts them into practice is like a wise man who built his house on the rock. The rain came down, the streams rose, and the winds blew and beat against that house; yet it did not fall, because it had its foundation on the rock."

—MATTHEW 7:24–25 (NIV)

The rain came down, the streams rose, and the winds blew . . . Life is uncertain, made up of good days and bad, joy and sorrow, certain steps and misadventures, but one thing remains constant: God is God, He is our Rock and our sure foundation. He will never change. He is the Master of the universe, the Beginning and the End, the Creator of all that is and will ever be. We are His creation and He loves us. Since the beginning of time, He had a plan for our life—an eternal plan that will carry out His will in the world. He wants us to know Him so we can serve Him.

As we hear Him speak, we discover His attributes through the sound of His voice. Though He may choose to speak to us like a whisper on the wind, He is still speaking. But God doesn't just speak to be heard. *He speaks to be obeyed.* His message is the same today as it was throughout the ages: "Whatever He says to you, do it" (John 2:5 NASB).

Build your house on the rock.

A Saint Speaks

"God chose not to reveal everything to us, but He has revealed some things to us. And a few things we know for sure. He always wants us to remember that He is God. He wants us to submit. He wants us to trust. He wants us to obey Him, just as Jesus did."

—LOIS EVANS

15

The Obedient Response

"Follow Me!"

—JOHN 21:19 (NASB)

Hemet, California, is a small city once known for its gangs, violence, and thriving drug business. The gang activity was so pervasive that it wasn't uncommon to see three generations of one family represented in the biggest group, the First Street Gang. The violence was so rampant that even police officers wouldn't go into the area without backup. There were nine methamphetamine labs in town, which supplied more than a million people a year.

The dominant religion was Scientology, and a meditation center at the center of town revealed the strong influence of New Age religion. Within the Christian community, there was a spirit of competition, particularly among the pastors. Hemet was the last place that most pastors wanted to minister. It was known as a pastor's graveyard.

When God called the Beckets to minister in Hemet, they didn't want to go. When they arrived, they didn't even unpack their bags in the hope that God would let them leave soon. But when God assured them that this was His calling on their lives, they knew that the only appropriate response would be complete obedience. To show their commitment, the Beckets bought ceme- tery plots. This was their way of saying, "Unless God tells us differently, we will die here."

In the years since the Beckets made a complete commitment to obey God, Hemet has completely changed. The First Street Gang has disbanded as its members have become saved. The drug trade has dropped by 75 per- cent. The New Age meditation center was destroyed by a fire—a fire that didn't destroy anything but the center itself. Cult membership has sunk to less than three-tenths of 1 percent of the population. The city's schools, which used to be the laughingstock of California, now have the highest scores and the lowest dropout rates. And churches and pastors aren't com- peting anymore. They are coming together to build the kingdom of God.

All of this because of a complete commitment to obedience!

The Beckets didn't give themselves an out. They didn't have another option waiting in the wings. They were fully surrendered to the plan of God, and unbelievable results followed.

God does not speak simply to be heard. He speaks to be obeyed. Obe- dience is the Alpha and Omega of discerning God's voice. It not only keeps the doors of communication open between you and God, but it's also the only appropriate response when He speaks. Being willing to obey begins the communication process; following through by actually obeying lays the groundwork for God to do incredible things in and through your life.

When God speaks to you, He is asking you to make a commitment. He wants your unquestioning, immediate commitment to obey what you hear. As you attempt to discern God's voice, are you willing to make this kind of commitment? If you aren't, God may choose not to speak to you. According to John 7:17, it is only the one who is willing to do the Father's will who can count on the Father revealing it.

A SAINT SPEAKS: *"His leading is only for those who are already committed to do as He may choose. To such it may be said: 'God is able to speak loud enough to make a willing soul hear.'"*

—LEWIS SPERRY CHAFER

An Unquestioning Commitment

God called Abraham His friend (James 2:23) not because he heard God's voice but because he was committed to obeying it without question. One of Abraham's most incredible acts of obedience came when God gave him some really bizarre instructions: "Take your only son—yes, Isaac, whom you love so much—and go to the land of Moriah. Sacrifice him there as a burnt offering on one of the mountains, which I will point out to you" (Genesis 22:2).

Abraham must have found God's request mind-boggling, not only because he loved Isaac, but also because God had promised him that He would make a great nation out of Isaac's descendants. What God was asking Abraham to do seemed irrational; worse, it seemed to contradict His own word. Yet, Abraham chose to obey, and as a result, he saw God's supernatural activity in his life.

I don't know about you, but I want to see God's supernatural activity in my life as well. I don't want to just hear about it in other people's lives and watch it from afar. I want to experience it. Over and over again, Scripture makes it clear that the prerequisite for experiencing God is obeying God. We must make obedience a habit.

> **A SAINT SPEAKS:** *"An important prerequisite to hearing God clearly is to have an open vertical relationship with the Lord and to be submitted to His plan for our lives. If there is unconfessed sin or continued disobedience in our lives, there will be a 'closed heaven' above us and a disruption in hearing from the Lord. God cannot draw near to us while we are walking away from Him through disobedience at the same time. With an 'open heaven' and a surrendered will, we will be able to clearly hear God's voice in our hearts."*
>
> —JIM CYMBALA

A couple of years ago, the Lord blessed me with a sweet friend, Mary Elaine. I treasure her for the impact that she has made on my spiritual life. She is a woman who sees the hand of God in her everyday existence. I have watched the Lord show up miraculously time and time again to provide for her family in big ways and small. Like the time she unexpectedly received scholarship money, at the last moment, to pay for her dyslexic son to attend a private school. While this is only one example of God's faithfulness, Mary Elaine has many stories about how the Lord has shown up in her life.

One day while we were having lunch together, we talked about why some believers like her seem to experience God's supernatural power more often than others. I wondered aloud why so many Christians often live their entire lives without witnessing God's handiwork.

Mary Elaine replied, "I think that God's supernatural activity is so evident in my life because I have decided the only appropriate response to Him is complete obedience. I am committed to obeying His leading no matter how absurd His instructions might seem to me."

This kind of complete, obedient response to God's leading allows Him to do incredible things in her life and all those who respond in this way.

Are you willing to respond to God in complete obedience, no matter how strange or absurd His instructions may seem? Often we are willing to obey God, but we want to have a fallback plan—just in case!

HE SPEAKS: *"His mother told the servants, 'Do whatever he tells you.'"*

—JOHN 2:5

In 1518, Hernán Cortés convinced the Spanish governor of Cuba to give him command of an expedition of eleven ships and six hundred men to establish a colony in Mexico. After a long voyage filled with hardships, they finally arrived at their destination. Cortés knew that his men wanted to return to Cuba, so to prevent that, he did the unthinkable: he burned the ships. Cortés was so committed to the task at hand that he closed all avenues of escape.

This is the type of obedience that God wants from us. He wants us to burn our ships and close all avenues of escape. He asks us to throw ourselves wholeheartedly into doing what He has asked of us. This requires radical faith and trust in God.

Scripture has a name for believers who always have an escape plan. They are called "double-minded" (James 4:8 NASB). Any believers who desire to hear from God—but have a "plan B" in their pocket—shouldn't "expect to receive anything from the Lord"—including His continued direction and guidance. He knows your heart and is totally aware of whether or not you have decided to obey Him, regardless of what His instructions are. If you aren't committed to obeying Him immediately and completely, He may choose not to speak.

If you aren't hearing from God, ask the Lord to reveal to you if double-mindedness is the cause. God wants you to throw yourself wholeheartedly into doing what He has asked of you. When you choose to obey, choose committed obedience.

When Abraham set out for Mt. Moriah to carry out the difficult instructions of Yaweh, he didn't take some sacrificial animal that he could substitute for Isaac at the last minute. During his seventy-two hour trip, he had plenty of time to change his mind, but he was committed to obeying the Lord completely and unquestioningly.

> **HE SPEAKS:** *"The Sovereign Lord has spoken to me, and I have listened. I do not rebel or turn away. . . . Therefore, I have set me face like a stone, determined to do his will. And I know that I will triumph."*
>
> —ISAIAH 50:5, 7

An Immediate Commitment

Abraham not only obeyed, but he obeyed without delay. In fact, every time God gave him instructions, he obeyed immediately. Take a look at his track record:

- When God told him to leave his homeland, Abraham set out (Genesis 12:1, 4).

- When God told him exactly what kind of offering to make Him, Abraham immediately did exactly what He asked (Genesis 15:9–10).

- When God gave him instructions to circumcise every male in his household, Abraham did it the very same day (Genesis 17:23).

- When God told him to sacrifice his son, he rose early the next morning to accomplish the task (Genesis 22).

Although Abraham wasn't perfect, he knew the importance of doing, without delay, what God asked him to do.

> **HE SPEAKS:** *"I will hurry, without lingering, to obey your commands."*
>
> —Psalm 119:60

Unlike Abraham, I probably would have waited at least a couple of days before sacrificing my son, to make sure I had heard God correctly. When the Lord gives me instructions that I don't particularly care for, or am afraid to carry out, the last thing I want to do is get up early in the morning to do it. I procrastinate. I often find myself thinking about it, praying about it, talking to friends about it, or even trying to ignore it. When instructions from God are difficult, as they often are, I'm often slow to obey.

Yet when God told him to do the unthinkable, Abraham immediately marched up a mountain. And because he obeyed immediately, he experienced God's divine intervention. I've always wondered, *Would that ram have been caught in that bush if Abraham had waited a day, week, or month to do what God told him?* God alone knows. What we do know is that because Abraham immediately obeyed, God's deliverance was waiting on the mountaintop when he arrived. He experienced God in a supernatural way because he obeyed right away.

> **A SAINT SPEAKS:** *"The worst thing you can do—the quickest way to become insensitive—is to ignore an impression. So you must commit yourself to listening to your Lord for the purpose of responding to what He says, and you must not allow yourself to hear without responding."*
>
> —PETER LORD

Several years ago, I fully intended to go back to Dallas Theological Seminary to get a doctoral degree. I'd been thinking about it for quite some time and had gone through the tedious, time-consuming admissions process. I spent many hours making sure that everything was filled out correctly before I packaged it all up and drove to the school to drop it off. I'll never forget the excitement I felt knowing that I would soon be back in school.

But while I was driving to the seminary to drop off my application, the Holy Spirit spoke clearly to my heart. *I didn't tell you that I wanted you back in school,* He said. *You want to be back in school, but I have other plans for you.*

This impression was so strong that I knew God was speaking to me. For a moment I thought about going ahead and dropping off the application and then talking it over with my husband when I got home. But then I remembered the principle of immediate obedience. I took the next exit off of the freeway and went straight back home. Within weeks, God began to weave a web of events that would lead to the ministry in which my husband and I are now engaged.

In all the years since then, I've never once had a desire to go back to school for that degree. God has completely removed the desire and replaced it with a desire for a ministry and a family. I didn't know at the time all that God had planned for me, but He knew, and my immediate obedience has paid off.

What might the Lord accomplish in and through you if you respond immediately to what He is asking you to do?

One afternoon I was thinking about the new office that the Lord was providing for Going Beyond Ministries. I thanked Him for His goodness to us. He had supernaturally provided the property for us and we were very grateful. But we had no money to buy desks, chairs, and the other office furniture we needed to equip the space. Around two o'clock in the afternoon, I asked the Lord if He would provide us with what we needed. That night a friend from church called with amazing news. A woman she knew had offered to give us a warehouse full of office furniture! A later conversation with this woman, whom I had never met, revealed that she had been standing in her storage unit at 2:00 p.m. that afternoon looking at all of the furniture she owned and wondering what to do with it. She thought about selling it but was prompted by the Lord to give it all away. Although her furniture was valuable and she was reluctant to give it away, she knew God was speaking, so she responded in complete, immediate obedience. Her generosity furnished our entire office, from top to bottom. Her radical obedience to God provided more than just furniture for a ministry, it gave me a renewed desire to respond to God fully as I clearly saw how obedience blesses others in our lives.

Why do we struggle against the leading of the One who knows exactly where we need to go and how we need to get there? Often it's because we think that we know better than He does. We're not willing to let go of the reins, so we struggle and pull and fight to go our own way. If we want to see God operating in our lives, we have to make a commitment to obey Him without question—immediately and completely—always keeping in mind all the other people our decision can affect.

> **A SAINT SPEAKS:** *"I know God is speaking to me when in spite of my initial struggle, there is an undeniable release and peace that follows when I have obeyed His voice. When I finally do the thing He has been nudging me to do, whether it's letting something or someone go, or taking a step toward the unknown, there is a deep calm in my soul. Where my heart and mind were once filled with terrible angst, I am now filled with a supernatural peace."*
>
> —KATHY TROCOLLI

As you have read this book and tried to follow its teaching, I hope you are more clearly able to hear and discern the things that God is telling you. If you have begun to look inward to the Spirit's impression on your conscience and sought confirmation through the Scriptures, I'm certain that you are hearing from God. What is the thing you sense the Lord is asking you to do today? What do you plan to do about it? My friend, when you hear God's voice saying, "Follow Me!" I urge you to heed it. Choose obedience today! I guarantee that the results will be glorious.

HOW DO YOU KNOW IT'S GOD'S VOICE?

"I know the Lord is speaking to me every time I read His Word or hear someone else read it. As Augustine said, 'When the Bible speaks, God speaks!' When I hear the Word preached, the preacher is merely an instrument through whom God wants to speak to my heart. When I open my Bible to read, God speaks to me. For most of us, the question isn't, 'Is God speaking to me?' The question is: 'Am I listening to Him speak? And am I responding to what He has said?'"

—NANCY LEIGH DEMOSS

The Sound of His Voice

"He is a God who is passionate about
his relationship with you."

—Exodus 34:14

A friend of mine and I were sitting in my living room talking about *Discerning the Voice of God.* She wanted to know what
I had learned from all my research and study. I told her that
what I've learned is that discerning God's voice is a lot simpler than I originally thought. *It's all about relationship.* The more
intimate your relationship with God, the more clearly you'll
discern His voice.

To picture the kind of intimate relationship the Lord wants
to have with us, Scripture compares it to the relationship between a shepherd and his sheep. This analogy doesn't resonate
with modern-day believers as it would have with the saints in
Bible times. Our unfamiliarity with an ancient shepherd's relationship with his sheep can cause us to miss the vital truth
Jesus was teaching.

I am continually amazed at the uncomplicated analogy
Jesus used to describe God's ongoing communication with His

people: "My sheep hear my voice; I know them, and they follow me" (John 10:27). There it is, plain and simple.

In Jesus' day, the communication a shepherd had with his sheep was based on the closeness of their relationship. Lambs learned to discern their shepherd's voice from others as they got to know him and practiced responding to his voice. Newborn lambs were less capable of distinguishing his voice than adult sheep were. They gained that skill over time. Eventually, the relationship became so close that when their shepherd called them, they understood exactly what he was saying and would follow him.

One of the greatest discoveries of my Christian life has been that *I can discern God's voice.* I no longer think that hearing the Lord's voice is for others but not for me. Learning that I can discern God's voice has filled me with a sense of anticipation I never had before. My life has become a glorious, supernatural adventure as I wait to hear from God day by day.

Do I sometimes make mistakes? I sure do! But that's how we become spiritually mature—by practicing listening to Him speak and obeying His instructions. I have learned the most about discerning God's voice from the mistakes I've made as I've tried to discern correctly. God graciously honors our heart's desire to obey even when we may be a little off base.

We can't separate discerning God's voice from our relationship with Him. Once we enter God's sheepfold and start to get to know Him, intimacy builds. Eventually we come to know Him so well that we can know if He is speaking simply by asking, "Does this sound like God's voice?" If it does, it will have the same characteristics you've read about in this book.

God's voice resonates within us because it speaks in a language that we, by the power of the Holy Spirit, can completely comprehend. It's a personal dialect designed to reveal His character so that we can know His will, desire it, and have the power to carry it out. This is the essence of discerning God's voice.

Hearing God's voice is impossible for someone who hasn't yet been born of the Spirit. It isn't enough to just be in the sheepfold. You have to be one of His sheep. You have to have a relationship with Him before you can discern His voice. Human intelligence and wisdom can't help an unregenerate soul discern God's voice. It's an act of the Spirit. We're born into the human family with physical ears, but when we're reborn into the family of God, we receive spiritual ears—the spiritual equipment necessary to hear spiritual things.

Friend, is Jesus your Shepherd? Have you placed your faith in Jesus Christ alone? If not, please know that God longs to have a relationship with you so He can speak to you. Listen, He's calling to you right now. Do you hear Him?

About the Author

Priscilla Shirer is a Bible teacher. She graduated from the University of Houston with a bachelor's degree in communications and from Dallas Theological Seminary with a master's degree in biblical studies.

For more than ten years Priscilla has been a conference speaker for major corporations, organizations, and Christian audiences across the United States and the world. Now in full-time ministry to women, Priscilla focuses on the expository teaching of the Word of God. She wants women to understand the uncompromising truths of Scripture and to be able to apply them to their lives in a practical way by the power of the Holy Spirit.

Priscilla is the author of *A Jewel in His Crown, A Jewel in His Crown Journal, And We Are Changed: Transforming Encounters with God,* and *He Speaks to Me: Preparing to Hear the Voice of God.* She is the daughter of pastor, speaker, and well-known author Dr. Tony Evans. She is married to her best friend, Jerry. The couple resides in Dallas, Texas, with their sons, Jackson and Jerry Jr.

Friend, how do you know for sure when God is speaking to you? I have asked many saints that very question, and I would like to hear your answer as well. You can reach me at:

Going Beyond Ministries
P.O. Box 2122
Cedar Hills, Texas 75106-2122
www.goingbeyond.com or www.priscillaspeaks.com

It's when you quiet your heart that

His voice becomes clear.

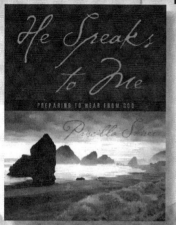

God lovingly and patiently waits to speak to us. But first, we have to still our hearts and prepare ourselves for His words. Simple to say, but often overlooked.

In Priscilla Shirer's six-week video teaching series, *He Speaks to Me: Preparing to Hear from God*, she relates important concepts from the beloved Bible account of the boy Samuel speaking with God. Six characteristics found in Samuel offer fresh insights into how we can listen for God's voice.

By listening to His voice and obeying Him, we will experience a closer relationship with God and a deeper desire to serve Him.

He Speaks to Me Member Book	1-4158-2093-7	**$10.95**
He Speaks to Me Leader Kit	1-4158-2094-5	**$149.95**
(2 DVDs and Member Book)		

Now Available

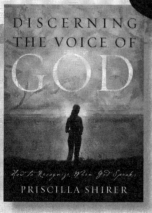

Discerning the Voice of God: How to Recognize When God Speaks by Priscilla Shirer

To order, visit **www.lifeway.com**, call **1.800.458.2772**, or visit the **LifeWay Christian Store** serving you. For more information on these Bible studies and exciting new events where Priscilla Shirer is speaking, visit **www.lifeway.com/women**.

LifeWay
Biblical Solutions for Life
WOMEN

A Jewel In His Crown

Rediscovering Your Value As a Woman of Excellence

ISBN-10: 0-8024-4083-5
ISBN-13: 978-0-8024-4083-9

When they become weary and discouraged, women lose sight of their real value as beloved daughters of God. *A Jewel in His Crown* examines how the way women view their worth deeply affects their relationships. This book teaches women how to renew strength and be women of excellence.

Priscilla Shirer herself is a crown jewel, mined from a family of precious gems. Reading her book is like a walk through Tiffany's as she uses her insight to draw the readers attention to the various facets of a godly woman's character. My prayer is that God will use A Jewel in His Crown *to help women embrace their primary aim of brining glory to God through the uniqueness of who they are in Christ.*

Anne Graham Lotz, AnGel Ministries